I0152093

# *No Compromise*

The Old Testament (I Chronicles 12:32) identified an especially wise tribe as "sons of Issachar." They were men who "understood the times and knew what Israel should do." Dr. Myers proves himself to be a modern-day member of that tribe with this excellent and encouraging book. He understands the times in which we live, and offers thoroughly biblical thinking about what we Christians should do. This short, highly readable book is nourishing both intellectually and spiritually.

-Warren Cole Smith
The Colson Center

I have been using devotionals in my morning quiet time for several years, this book, *No Compromise*, is filled with reflections and short stories that are among the best and most inspirational of those I have ever read. It is filled with encouraging axioms, inspirational anecdotes, soul-stirring scriptures, proverbs and principles to replenish a believers' virtue when our fire needs a fresh breeze to set it ablaze. After fueling our spirit during a time of daily Bible reading, just one short story or devotional is an excellence ignition source to set our souls on fire to go forth and glorify God for another day. This book will be a blessing to many.

-Dr. Kelvin J. Cochran, Chief Operating Officer,
Elizabeth Baptist Church
Former Atlanta Fire Chief

Your interest will be piqued and your heart encouraged as you read *No Compromise*. Dr. Myers' stories from history and current events, along with his own life experiences, will encourage you to anchor your trust in Jesus Christ and challenge you to live courageously for Him.

-Terry D. Smith
District Superintendent
Eastern PA District of the Christian and Missionary Alliance


This encouraging book equips readers to rest in God's objective view of life's practical issues rather than man's subjective points of view. *No Compromise* is a handbook of proper perspectives and wise insights for experiencing the abundant life.


-Trace Embry
Executive Director
Shepherd's Hill Academy


Dr. Myers has wonderfully woven God's love, mercy, and grace throughout this book. The stories are certain to cause mind and heart to desire more intimacy with our loving God, as it did for me. I will purchase and send copies of this gem to others!

-Dr. Ray Kincaid
Chief Executive Officer
Rego Designs

Dr. Myers has an amazing personal background...police officer, detective, University Vice President, and now President of Toccoa Falls College. He has uniquely taken his many life experiences using the Psalms, Proverbs and Parables from the infallible Word of God to teach the reader lessons for Daily Godly Living.

-John W. Allen,
Attorney

Reading Dr. Myers' book is a richly satisfying experience. His observations on popular culture are the product of his ability to view life through the lens of a biblical worldview. Written in an engaging style, *No Compromise* provides the reader with the conversational ammunition needed to engage secular culture with a winsome voice. Christians will be well served by this book because its contents are both urgent and timely.

-Dr. Brett Andrews
Dean of Business
Newman University

# No Compromise

## Thoughts from a Christian College President

by

**Dr. Robert M. Myers**

President
Toccoa Falls College,
Toccoa Falls, GA

Lantern Hollow Press

Lynchburg, VA

---

Library of Congress Control Number: 2017901688

Self Help/Motivational & Inspirational

Myers, Robert, 1957-
No Compromise: Thoughts from a Christian College President/ Robert Myers

A series of meditations on Christianity, its role in culture, and the state of common sense in America.

Includes bibliographic references.

ISBN-13: 978-0692842447 (Lantern Hollow Press)
ISBN-10: 0692842446

---

This book is dedicated to…


All those who realize that biblical truth requires no compromise.

# Foreword

We all jammed into the courtroom waiting for our names to be called as we hoped for a deferment from jury duty. We waited patiently as the judge called each person to come forward and plead their case.

When I approached the bench, I explained to the judge that I was scheduled for six days of performances. The judge was not impressed and told me to sit down. All of a sudden it hit me. Everyone had a story to tell. All of us had packed our schedules so full that we did not allow time for anything to interrupt our routines. Since the judge was unimpressed with my pleading, what was I to do?

As I sat in the jury room, I opened Dr. Myers' book and began to read. Then it happened. From the time I opened this amazing book to the time I finished the final story, I was hooked. I looked around at all those waiting in the jury room and wished that everyone had a copy of this book.

After finishing *No Compromise*, one word came to mind. That word was 'real'. In a world that is continually moving away from Godly principles, Dr. Myers reminds us to stay honest and true to God. I was reminded that being a follower of Christ is not just about words, it is about our actions. Dr. Myers is very candid about the importance of remaining faithful and loyal to the principles of the Word of God. He challenges us to go beyond what we know and step out on faith to become everything God has created us to be.

We must choose to be encouragers rather than critics. We must become Godly energy sources that sincerely recognize something special in everyone. This book is filled with stories about some very special people. Whether it is the sweet lady who offers someone a cold drink or another woman who is dancing to the music in the airport, we must take time to notice those around us and realize that God is using them to brighten our days and give us hope.

Dr. Myers is that special someone who always finds the good in everyone. I can best describe him as a spiritual cheerleader. Through his own personal testimony that he shares often, Dr. Myers has tapped into the true meaning of grace and redemption.

A few months ago, I had the honor and privilege of receiving an Honorary Doctorate Degree in Divinity from Toccoa Falls College. On graduation day, I watched Dr. Myers personally hand out each diploma to every student who walked through the line. He either shook their hands or gave them a big hug. What impressed me the most was how he had such encouraging words for every student. He knew them personally. It was obvious that he had invested in their lives. The love and respect for Dr. Myers from the student body that graduation day literally brought me to tears. You will receive a good dose of his heart from reading this book.

Whether you are sitting at home, your office, on a plane, or maybe awaiting jury duty, you will be blessed as you journey through each individual story that Dr. Myers so eloquently shares.

Those stories calmed my hectic life on that particular summer day while sitting at that courthouse. Even though I was not chosen for jury duty that week, I realize there will be many other times when I may stress over unexpected situations that will not fit into my busy schedule. This book reminded me that God is in control and everything will always work out for my good. I was so thankful for this consistent reminder from the very first story to the last.

As you read this book be encouraged and remember that although culture shifts, there is no compromise when it comes to following Christ!


Karen Peck

*Karen Peck and New River*

Thank you to Brian and Kami Melton from
Lantern Hollow Press


Rachel Burkholder, who edited this book


And for my favorite three non-stop thinkers who constantly
provide me with great topics:

Cheri Myers

Josh Myers

Joy Myers

# Preface

When you watch the news or monitor other media reports you find a world of critics. Everyday there are those pointing an accusing finger at someone else.

This book was written from a different perspective. This book is intended to be an encouragement. *No Compromise* contains a variety of stories. Some of these stories are about people making a difference in our world. Some folks made a positive impact on our world, while others did quite the opposite.

Some stories contain issues related to culture – issues that highlight the importance of not compromising on biblical principles. Still other stories detail compromises and the aftermath of poor choices.

As you read this book, ask yourself if cultural correctness has influenced your life in a negative way. Have you compromised on biblical standards? If so, it is time to realign your thoughts and life direction. Get back to the course God laid out for you.

While reading this book, be encouraged. You are not alone in whatever you are facing today. As Joshua 1:9 tells us:

*Be strong and courageous…*

May this book build your strength and help you realize the importance of *No Compromise* on biblical principles.

Dr. Robert M. Myers

# Table of Contents

# Contains No Butter

Truthful marketing and advertising has always been of interest to me. Recently, I was reading a label on a bottle of pancake syrup just thinking about the marketing approach this particular company was taking. As I read the label I noticed something very interesting. The label advertised the syrup as *Butter Rich*. In fact these two words were boldly written in bright blue letters across the front of the bottle. Looking at those two words I could just imagine a large stack of pancakes with melted butter and *butter rich* syrup running down the sides of the pancakes. Sounds good doesn't it?

There is just one problem. In small letters along the bottom of the syrup label are the following words: *contains no butter*. That's right...the butter rich advertising on the label is on a product that contains no butter. I'm not sure how something can be buttery rich with no butter but that is a problem for another day.

What this syrup label made me think about are labels. Specifically, the label many of us have attached to us that says *follower of Christ*. People are watching us to see if we live up to our advertising. Are we really the person we say we are? As I interact with folks all over the country I am saddened to see some who wear this label but probably should add some small print to their label that says, *contains no Christ*.

Most of us get frustrated when we believe we have been victims of false advertising. I suspect we also do great damage to the cause of Christ when we label ourselves as followers of Christ but when others observe our behavior they see no evidence of truth in our advertising.

I'm reminded of Matthew 7:17-20 that says:

> A good tree produces good fruit, and a bad tree produces bad fruit. A good tree can't produce bad fruit, and a bad tree can't produce good fruit. So every tree that does not produce good fruit is chopped down and thrown into the fire. Yes, just as you can identify a tree by its fruit, so you can identify people by their actions.

If you are wearing a *follower of Christ* label, make sure that you have truth in your advertising. Let others identify you as a follower of Christ by your actions, those actions that follow scripture. Let's not disappoint others and harm the cause of Christ by any false advertising.

# After the Mistake

It is common to think about past mistakes. While some of us focus on the past, others look to the future with excitement. These folks focusing on the future see a clean slate with new opportunities.

Recently I was listening to Jon Simeon talk about his job. Now if you are trying to rack your brain figuring out who Jon Simeon is and what books he has published you can just stop now. You have probably never heard about him before today.

Jon Simeon is an Alaska State Trooper. He is one of about eighty Alaska State Wildlife Troopers who patrol the entire state of Alaska. Jon deals with a lot of folks who make mistakes…big ones… just as any law enforcement officer does. However, in passing, Jon made this statement. Here is what he said:

> Mistakes happen all the time but it's what you do after the mistake that counts (National Geographic).

Let me say this again so it sinks in. Mistakes happen all the time but it's what you do after the mistake that counts.

Trooper Simeon hit the nail on the head with this statement. We all need to acknowledge that mistakes happen in our lives. Mistakes have occurred and they will again. The true mark of character is what you do after the mistake.

Everyday police officers see people make mistakes and then try to conceal what they did. Rather than simply admitting the mistake, the lies begin in an attempt to conceal the poor choice. Many of us do the same thing in our daily lives. We make a mistake and then look for ways to blame others, hide the action, minimize it, or look for some way to save face.

I am reminded of a verse in Proverbs.

> People who conceal their sins will not prosper, but if they confess and turn from them, they will receive mercy (Proverbs 28:13).

Let us all realize that we're going to make mistakes. It is going to happen. So, start focusing on what you will do after the mistake is made. Do what Proverbs instructs. Confess your mistakes to whomever you offended, ask for forgiveness from the person you offended, ask for God's forgiveness, and learn not to make the same mistake again.

If we will all do this, we will receive mercy, we will spend less time fretting about our mistakes, those around us will respect us for our truthfulness; we can focus on what is ahead rather than what is in our past.

# Oh, I Know That

I recently watched a video by Mark Dice that left me just shaking my head in despair. Let me set the stage for this video. Mark was walking on a pier in California checking on people's knowledge of both American history as well as basic listening skills. His question to everyone he stopped was this:

Why do we celebrate the 4th of July?

Pretty simple question, right? Not so fast. As you watch the video you will hear folks say that we declared our independence from China. Others thought we declared our independence from Mexico. Some thought Jesse Ventura signed our Declaration of Independence. Others thought Jack Lemmon signed it.

When was the Declaration of Independence signed? Some of the responses were 1974, 1976, 1978, 1762, 1812, and 1842. One woman said she has no hard feelings against the Mexicans since we have now declared our independence from them on July 4th.

What about listening skills? On the video you can hear Mark say this:

When the founding fathers signed the Declaration of Independence on July 4th, 1776…what date did they sign the Declaration of Independence (Dice)?

The answers ranged from, *I don't know*, to *19 something* and the list goes on (Dice).

Even when people hear the truth they don't recognize it. It's no wonder so many folks fall for any story they hear. Political stories? Sure we believe it. Lectures in the classroom supporting evolution? Sure. Why not? Abortion doesn't take a life? We can believe that one too.

The sonnet mounted on the Statue of Liberty reads:

> Give me your tired, your poor, your huddled masses...

Maybe we should add give us your ridiculous story too. We believe almost anything. A lack of knowledge combined with a lack of common sense is catastrophic but so very common.

In the Bible, the book of Proverbs says:

> Only simpletons believe everything they're told! The prudent carefully consider their steps (14:15).

Let us be counted among the folks with some common sense.

# Happy Birthday to Me

Suppose you have a birthday coming up. What is the one question everyone asks you? I suspect it is this question: *What do you want for your birthday?* When it is our birthday, most of us start thinking weeks ahead of our birthday for that perfect gift. We may hint about the gift to our family and friends or just blurt out what we really want.

Let me tell you about a man who has taken a different approach to his birthday celebration. Instead of focusing on what he can *get* for his birthday this man decided to *give* gifts on his birthday.

Bob Blackley, from North Carolina, spends his birthday standing at an intersection giving away money. He does it every year. This year Bob celebrated his 59th birthday by standing at a busy street corner holding a cardboard sign that reads:

> I have a home,
> I have a job
> Could you use an extra $5.00?

Bob passed out $800 dollars to one hundred and sixty people who drove by (Hennessey).

What a different perspective than the one pervasive in our culture. In a world of what's in it for me, Bob looked at how he could celebrate by serving others.

I am reminded of someone else who lived an earthly life of service…Jesus. Remember the time when Jesus learned about the death of John the Baptist? The Book of Matthew tells us that Jesus went to a quiet place to be alone but the crowds still followed

Him. Jesus couldn't find any peace and quiet. His disciples told Jesus to send the crowds away so they could go and buy food. That would give Jesus a chance for the solitude He wanted.

Rather than an inward, selfish focus, the scriptures tell us that Jesus was concerned for the people in the crowd and fed them. In fact, He fed them in a miraculous way. With five loaves and two fish Jesus fed over 5,000 people that day. No inward focus for Jesus but rather a deep concern for others.

Am I saying don't enjoy your birthday and the gifts you receive? Of course not. What I am saying is don't forget in all you do to focus on serving others. There are a lot of folks who are struggling daily and just need you, through your actions, to remind them that Jesus loves them. You can show the love of Christ in a tangible way by simply focusing on others.

# A Punch in the Stomach

When is the last time you got a good punch in the stomach? A punch that you didn't see coming…it just blindsided you. It left you bent over trying to catch your breath. I'm not talking about a physical punch. I'm talking about an emotional punch.

Some of you might be suffering from one of those punches right now. Have you been hit by a health issue, an issue with your spouse, an issue with your children, depression, or one of many other emotional attacks? If you have, I promise that you're not the only one facing such an issue.

Sometimes we believe that if we follow Christ life will be only happiness and problems will just disappear. Well, that is certainly never promised in scripture. As believers, we face all sorts of disappointments and struggles…it's just a part of living. So, as believers in Christ, how do we handle these situations? What defense do we have to counter these emotional punches?

Let me tell you in one word what we have. We have *hope*. But I don't mean hope in the context used by so many today such as, I hope my favorite football team wins. I hope my hair turns out right. I hope my Thanksgiving turkey is perfect. I hope I get a raise. No…I mean we have a different kind of hope.

The hope I'm talking about is the hope found in Romans 12:12. Here is what it says:

> Rejoice in our confident hope. Be patient in trouble and keep on praying.

What is our confident hope? It is our hope in an all powerful, loving God. In fact, Romans 15:13 takes this issue of hope and puts it in perspective. Here's what we read there:

I pray that God, the source of hope, will fill you completely with joy and peace because you trust in him. Then you will overflow with confident hope through the power of the Holy Spirit.

So today place your hope in God and I pray that your pain will turn to joy and peace.

# I Know My Way

I decided to visit a restaurant near the town where I live. When I left the restaurant to head home, I was certain I knew the way. I looked at my GPS, decided not to turn it on, and headed home. But late at night, after driving far too long on winding country roads, I realized that I had turned the wrong way out of the restaurant parking lot. Even though I was certain I knew my way home I didn't even make the correct turn out of the parking lot.

Almost daily folks, who are positive about their spiritual direction in life, confront me with questions and opinions. Some folks are positive there are no absolute truths in this world. In a recent conversation, someone displayed their lack of critical thinking when they told me they did not believe any absolute truth existed. When I asked them if they were sure they replied *absolutely!* Yes, you read that correctly, these folks were absolutely sure that absolute truth did not exist.

Yet, absolute truth exists all around us. There are absolute truths in mathematics, music, science, and the list could go on. If we didn't believe that these truths existed, why would we spend our time and money to study at colleges and universities? Our very diplomas signify that we have mastered a variety of absolute truths.

When it comes to issues of spirituality, suddenly the rules change. Our compartmentalized worldview can accept absolute truths in math and science but when it comes to God we question how truth can possibly exist. I hear folks frequently question the existence of the God of the Bible, yet I see few of these folks truly seeking evidence. You see, when it comes to God and absolute truth, the discussions generally revolve around heated opinions. We seldom bring discussions centered on opinions to reasonable conclusions. Could you imagine courtrooms that simply accepted everyone's opinion?

So today, I challenge both believers in Christ and non-believers. What evidence would it take to convince you of the existence of the God of the Bible? Begin gathering your evidence. For believers in Christ, it is important to have an answer for your beliefs and the evidence you collect is critical. I hear many folks say they believe in God because the Bible commands it. However, what evidence supports the Bible? If you were talking to a non-believer about the Bible, what historical, archeological, or physical evidence would you provide as proof of Biblical truths?

For non-believers you just might be surprised where the evidence takes you. Instead of simply giving an opinion on Biblical and spiritual issues start compiling the evidence for yourself. Are you looking for a few books to get started? Try some of these:

*The Case for Christ* by Lee Stroebel
*Is the Bible True…Really?* by Josh McDowell
*Cold Case Christianity: A Homicide Detective Investigates the Claims of the Gospel* by J. Warner Wallace.

Remember, you may truly believe you know your way home when it comes to spiritual issues but you may be merrily driving down the wrong road.

# I'll Take You to the Moon

History records that many of our founding fathers and prominent historical figures had a love for the God of the Bible. Do you remember the words Francis Scott Key wrote as part of the fourth verse of the Star Spangled Banner? In case you forgot, here is a portion of what Francis Scott Key wrote:

> Then conquer we must, when our cause it is just,
> And this be our motto: "In God is our trust."

Let's talk about another prominent American hero who had a love for God...Astronaut Buzz Aldrin. July 21, 2014 marked the forty-fifth anniversary of the first manned landing on the moon. Mission commander Neil Armstrong was the first to walk on the moon and was followed out of the lunar module by Buzz Aldrin who became the second man to walk on the moon.

Aldrin did something very special when he and Armstrong landed the lunar module on the moon. Aldrin had communion. During the radio blackout in the lunar module, while things were quiet, he opened the communion elements and celebrated communion right there...just before stepping onto the surface of the moon. As Aldrin took communion, he read this verse from John 15:5:

> I am the vine, you are the branches. Whoever remains in me, and I in him, will bear much fruit; for you can do nothing without me ("Guidepost Classics").

Aldrin later said this about the experience of communion on the moon:

It was interesting to think that the very first liquid ever poured on the moon and the first food eaten there, were communion elements ("Guidepost Classics").

It's not the act of taking communion that makes this important. It's the fact that Aldrin took time to honor his God for all God had done in his life. Look at the verse from the Book of John that Aldrin chose to read during his communion time...*for you can do nothing without me*. It is very clear that the man who was about to leave the lunar module and walk on the moon recognized that he could do nothing without God. What a remarkable way for Aldrin to thank God for what God had done in Aldrin's life.

So...don't be fooled by the minority of folks who say our country had no historical roots with the God of the Bible. Francis Scott Key and Buzz Aldrin would tell them they are wrong.

# Can Worry Add Years to Your Life?

Much of my traveling involves sitting in airports waiting for flights. On a recent trip, I found myself at the Denver airport. All of a sudden a very large storm blew over the airport. Paper and cardboard were being blown all over the runways. Huge dark clouds covered the airport and all flights were immediately held for a weather delay. If you have flown before, you know that when you have weather like this you usually have a pretty rough ride after takeoff.

When we finally boarded the plane and were ready to taxi down the runway, the pilot's voice came on the intercom and told us to expect a rough flight as we went through the storm. The lady across the aisle from me suddenly looked sick. In fact, she stopped the flight attendant and asked if there was a place for her to lie down. I watched the flight attendants clear three seats so she could rest. Now prior to the pilot's announcement she looked just fine to me.

Well, the pilot was right. It was a pretty rough flight heading through the storm but after about thirty minutes of getting roughed up a bit, something really miraculous happened. Suddenly we were in beautiful sunlight watching the dark clouds disappear below us. The flight smoothed out, sunshine was flowing in through the windows and there were only blue skies. We left the terrible storm far below us.

Now as I think of the storm and of the woman on the plane I described earlier, I can't help but think about our daily lives. We have life storms that blow into our lives very quickly: health storms, financial storms, family storms, and the list is endless. All of a sudden, like the woman on the plane, we aren't feeling very well. We begin to worry and we're looking around for a place to lie down and fret. We spend our time worrying about things that will never happen. Imagine if you could total all the time in your life you spent worrying about things that never happened. What a waste of our time. As my son often says around our house, *don't borrow trouble from tomorrow*. Let's change our perspective on life and stop worrying about things that probably will never happen. Scripture makes it very clear. In Matthew 6:27 we read:

Can all your worries add a single moment to your life?

Let me answer that for you. No they can't. So...put your worries behind you, put on your seat belt, put on the armor of God, and watch the storm clouds disappear as you fly into the sunlight of God's plan for your life.

# I'm Fine

I am about to point out one of the biggest lies told in America today. It is a question followed by an answer. Are you ready? Here is the question, *How are you?* Here is the answer, *fine.*

How many times in your day do you ask that question more as a greeting than a question? In fact, most of us probably wouldn't know what to do if the response was anything other than *fine.* Often we don't even stop to really hear the answer. We pass people on the street, in the office, in church and say, *How are you?* and keep walking hearing a faint *fine* coming from somewhere behind us.

The other day, I was walking down the sidewalk and asked our question to a young lady, *How are you?* What do you think was the response? Of course...*fine.* So I stopped and asked this lady how she really was doing. This lady's eyes filled with tears and she began to tell me the story of a life that was unraveling. We actually had a chance to talk about life, about things that mattered to her. I really just needed to listen and she did most of the talking.

I am reminded of the care Christ showed for others. I think of the story in the book of John telling us about the woman at the well. Christ could have ignored her. In fact, she was a Samaritan and Jews usually did not associate with Samaritans. If Christ wanted to be polite He could have simply asked how she was doing as He hurried past. I bet you her answer would have been *fine* even though she was deeply suffering. Yet Christ stopped because He really cared about her and engaged her in meaningful discussion about her soul.

May I ask you to start investing more time with others? Listen to what people really have to say. Talk with them. Care about them. Christ would ask us to do nothing less.

# Check Engine Light

Having car problems is just annoying. I was talking with a friend the other day who said that while he was driving his *check engine* light came on. My friend pulled to the side of the road and just couldn't figure out what was happening to his car. His car gave him an option of running a diagnostic to determine the problem.

As we were talking about this it struck me that sometimes God causes the spiritual *check engine* light to come on in our lives. Often when it does we experience the same panic that sets in when it happens to our car. When God sets off the spiritual *check engine* light, we stop what we are doing and try to figure out what is happening in our lives…we run a diagnostic.

Some of you are experiencing an event in your life right now that has activated your spiritual *check engine* light. It might be a financial issue, an issue with your marriage or a relationship, or even a medical issue. Whatever the cause, your situation is something that has caused you to pull over and run a diagnostic on your life.

May I tell you that spiritual diagnostics are a good thing? Sometimes we all need to pull onto the shoulder of the road and take a break from our normal routines. These diagnostic times are often the moments that God speaks to us if we will simply listen. But…the key is we must be willing to listen.

I think about the life of Saul of Tarsus. I think we could all agree that the *check engine* light was activated in his life. Here is a man moving through life as usual, eager to kill followers of God at every possible opportunity. The Bible tells us that Saul suddenly saw a light from heaven and God actually spoke to Saul asking why he was persecuting God's followers. In the middle of all this, Saul was instantly struck blind. I think it is safe to say that Saul was pulled off to the side of the road with his *check engine* light activated. We know that Saul was doing a spiritual diagnostic because the Bible tells us that when this event occurred, he was busy praying (Acts 9).

Running a spiritual diagnostic by stopping and listening to God changed a persecutor into an apostle. By stopping to listen to God's instructions Saul's life was changed forever.

What about you today? Are you disabled on the side of the road with your *check engine* light activated? May I encourage you to complete a spiritual diagnostic and see what it would take for you to get moving again…this time with a changed and renewed life. Like Saul, your life or situation may be changed in a moment by listening to the instructions that God is giving you.

# The Heart Wants What It Wants

I was reading an article titled, *Couple Has An Open Marriage So Complicated It's Hard to Keep Track*. This article discussed the lives of Michael, his wife, Kamala, their six-year-old son, and Michael's live in girlfriend, Rachel. Kamala is also in a relationship with someone other than Michael. Now you can better understand the title of the article.

Author Jenny Block, who commented on this story, had some surprising thoughts in support of this type of lifestyle. Block said this:

> We cannot control our own desires and we certainly cannot control the desires of others (Wong).

Really? We cannot control our own desires? That is a rather broad and flawed statement.

We control our own desires everyday and I suspect Jenny Block does too. If we didn't have the ability to control our own desires, we would drive whatever speed we chose rather than obey the speed limit. In stores, we would push people out of our way in the checkout line rather than show patience. We would eat everything in sight rather than show discretion. If we wanted something in the store we would just take it rather than pay for it. It is absurd to say that we cannot control our own desires. Each of us chooses to control our own desires every day.

Block also said this, *the heart wants what it wants,* again insinuating that we are all so weak that we can't control ourselves. Block makes it sound as though we get an impulse to react in some manner and we just must comply. We simply can't stop ourselves. What a poor excuse for choosing your lifestyle. Notice I said choosing a lifestyle because that is exactly what each of us does. People could certainly choose a monogamous heterosexual lifestyle, they have the control to do so, but instead they choose other alternatives.

Stop playing the victim with lifestyle decisions. Each of us makes the choice; the way you live isn't forced upon you. Instead of saying, like Jenny Block, *the heart wants what the heart wants*, how about following some Biblical advice found in Proverbs 4:23 that says:

> Guard your heart above all else, for it determines the course of your life.

Don't follow ridiculous desires of your heart. Guard your heart from absurd decisions, show restraint and integrity and live the way God intended for you to live.

# That Scares Me

We live in a world that is full of evil. Events often unfold that leave us confused and often fearful. But let me take you to an event that may help us all work through the variety of world issues that can leave us worried and fearful. Let me take you to the Christmas story...specifically to the story of the shepherds.

As you recall from the book of Luke, a group of shepherds were watching their sheep in the field. Suddenly, an angel appeared and according to the Bible, the shepherds were terrified. You see it's not just present day folks who are scared of unexpected events. It is part of human nature to be frightened about things we don't understand. But what did the angel say to the shepherds? It was a simple message. Here it is:

> Don't be afraid...I bring you good news that will bring great joy to all people. The Savior – yes the Messiah, the Lord - has been born today in Bethlehem (Luke 2:9-10).

The issue of fear is one we all face; from the shepherds in the Christmas story to all of us who now get real-time media reports of the terrible events taking place throughout the world. Yet again, the Bible cautions us about this spirit of fear. The book of II Timothy 1:7 tells us:

> For God has not given us a spirit of fear and timidity, but of power, love, and self-discipline.

With the birth of our Savior, we can triumph over fear. Let me again repeat the same message delivered to the shepherds. *Don't be afraid...the Savior has been born today in Bethlehem.* We serve a risen Savior, Jesus Christ who has dominion over fear. Nothing that the world can produce surprises Christ.

So celebrate in the joy of knowing that our Savior has given us a spirit of power, not fear. Rejoice in our Savior who has already defeated the power of fear and instead brought us power, love, and great joy.

# Common Sense: Rest in Peace

Two years ago former U.S. Congressman Anthony Weiner was accused of sending a sexually suggestive photograph from his twitter account. The photo was sent to a twenty-one year old college student from Seattle, Washington. This young college student was one of many who followed Weiner's twitter posts.

Initially, it was reported that Weiner denied sending the picture and blamed the photo on others who were trying to discredit him.

Shortly after, a second woman came forward with sexually suggestive material that she said was sent to her by Weiner. As the evidence began to mount against him, ABC News, Politico, and other news sources reported these statements from Weiner:

> I have not been honest with myself, my family, my constituents, my friends and supporters, and the media and to be clear, the picture was of me, and I sent it (CNN).

Weiner is also reported to have said he had engaged in several inappropriate conversations conducted over Twitter, Facebook, email and occasionally on the phone and had exchanged messages and photos of an explicit nature with about six women over the last three years. On June 16, 2011, Weiner resigned his seat in Congress (Hall).

CNN reported that just over a month after entering New York City's high-profile mayoral race in 2013, Anthony Weiner moved ahead for the first time in the crowded Democratic primary and was actually leading in the polls at one point. Weiner was again involved in politics.

So, we had a congressman who engaged in inappropriate sexual behavior and then lied when he was caught. Later, the people of New York City supported him in his new quest to become mayor. Do you ever find yourself just shaking your head and wondering what ever happened to common sense? Most of us would never hire someone like Weiner for our businesses yet some folks will elect him to run their city.

I am reminded of James 1:5 that says this:

> If you need wisdom, ask our generous God, and he will give it to you.

Perhaps many in our country should ask for a liberal dose of wisdom.

# Comparing Yourself to Others

I have been noticing all the mini storage facilities that are popping up all over America. Have you seen them? Rows of little storage units with a catchy name often next to a major road. Wherever I travel I am certain to pass multiple rental facilities where you can easily store all your excess stuff. You can rent spaces of various sizes or even choose the nice climate controlled storage units. Have you ever wondered why we are seeing all these storage units?

As I thought more about all our excess stuff that we need to store, I started to wonder if we aren't going through life comparing ourselves to others. My neighbor has a new motorcycle so I need one too. How about that nice pool table? I better get one of those. I wouldn't want anyone to think less of me because I don't have the same stuff that everyone else does.

Eventually we all end up with way too many possessions to keep in our house and we need the services of the mini storage facilities. We have so much useless stuff that we now need to pay to store it. We not only have excess stuff, we also have a monthly storage bill so we may keep the items we don't even need.

Do you ever compare yourself to others? Do you ever wonder why you don't have all the stuff others do? Do you wonder why you aren't as smart as someone else? Do you wonder why you aren't as handsome or pretty as other people? I think we all do. The problem with comparing yourself to others is that it only does harm to you. Why would we even think of using others as a standard of measurement to determine our worth? It makes no sense but yet we do it every day.

Here is what the Bible says about these comparisons. In 2 Corinthians 10:12 we find this:

> Oh, don't worry; we wouldn't dare say that we are as wonderful as these other men who tell you how important they are! But they are only comparing themselves with each other, using themselves as the standard of measurement. How ignorant!

You see, God made you just the way you are. You are unique...a one-of-a-kind. So be yourself. Instead of using other people as your standard of measure for your worth, use the scriptures. If you measure up there, I bet you won't need the services of the mini storage facilities. I bet your life even begins to take on a different set of priorities.

Next time you drive by a mini storage facility, remember not to be tempted to compare yourself to others. God made you to just be you.

# Dealing with the Unexpected

Not long ago I decided to tackle a job I was dreading. I had several trees that had fallen in my yard and it was time to cut them up and split the wood. I got out my chain saw, filled it with gasoline and bar oil, put on my safety equipment and was ready to start. The job I had been dreading was finally getting done. I started the chainsaw and made my first cut. I was about halfway through the cut when the tree shifted in a direction I hadn't expected. Not a big shift...just enough to pinch the chainsaw blade. In other words, the chainsaw was now pinched between the tree and the piece of wood I was cutting and I couldn't get the chainsaw out. It was stuck in the tree. Suddenly, work stopped. I hadn't expected this.

I spent a considerable amount of time trying to insert wedges, to reposition a tree, which I discovered I really couldn't move, and became frustrated at being forced to deal with the unexpected. The plans I made for the day were falling apart. Things just weren't working like I had planned.

How about you? Do you think you have your life planned? Do you think you have everything calculated and life is going to progress just as you have it planned? Well, get ready. I can guarantee that something is going to pinch your chainsaw blade. You will run into health issues, marriage difficulties, problems with your children, financial problems, or a host of other blade pinchers. I'm not saying this to scare you. I'm simply saying this because it's usually how life works.

For believers in Christ, we have a wonderful promise when we are confronted with these life pinchers. In I Peter 5:7 we read:

> Give all your worries and cares to God, for He cares about you.

Did you hear that? Give all your worries and cares to God, for He cares for you. Don't give some of your worries but give all of your worries. Not some of the things that are bothering you but all of them. When something happens to pinch your life, remember this promise and do it...give your worries and cares to God.

But let's not forget the second part of this verse. We're not told just to give our worries to God, we're told to give our worries to God because He cares for us. What a wonderful promise. In times of difficulty we serve a God who actually cares for us and desires to take our cares and worries away from us...to relieve that pinch we are feeling.

So instead of becoming frustrated and upset with unexpected situations in your life, take this promise to heart and give your cares to God because He cares for you. See what a difference this one action makes in your life.

# Developing Godly Character: The Gift of Thankfulness

So many people today feel entitled rather than thankful. In fact, in the December 12, 2013 edition of USA today there appears an interesting story. A sixteen-year-old boy was arrested and accused of killing four pedestrians while he was driving drunk. His defense? Affluence. Dr. Gary Buffone, a psychologist, explains this term:

> …used to describe a condition in which children — generally from richer families — have a sense of entitlement, are irresponsible, [and] make excuses for poor behavior… (Plushnick-Mash)

This young man was hoping to receive a lighter punishment because he was so accustomed to doing whatever he pleased that he should not be held accountable for making a poor choice.

Let me contrast this story with that of the life of Abigail Smith. Abigail was a twenty-four year old young woman who, in 2012, was diagnosed with a very rare form of cancer. When her doctor gave her the news, he said this:

> Everyone is dealt a deck of cards. We don't get to choose the cards, but we do get to choose how we play them. We can either be bitter or thankful.

Abby chose thankfulness. She underwent surgery and thirty-seven radiation treatments. Eventually, there was nothing else that could medically stop the cancer from spreading. Abigail was going to die.

You might think that Abigail became bitter or lived hoping for a miracle but here is what Abigail said:

> Miracles are a temporary fix. They are only a shadow of things to come. I don't need a miracle to know that God loves me (Orme, "Abby").

In a video that documents Abigail's story, she said, *Live one day at a time and live each day to the fullest*. Then she said thank you to those who were involved in her life. Abigail chose to be thankful despite living through a year of pain and suffering. Abigail died in December of 2013 still thankful for a remarkable life, for family, friends, and a God who loved her.

So we have a choice. Live suffering from affluence or live joyfully with thanksgiving. I hope you choose thankfulness.

# Developing Godly Character:
# The Gift of Patience

We live in a world where most people expect things right away. We have microwaves that make our meals in only a few minutes. We enjoy fast food, express lanes in the grocery store, instant streaming of movies, we have instant foods ranging from instant coffee to instant rice. We become frustrated when life isn't so instant and we find ourselves in a traffic jam, delayed by road construction, waiting for a table at a restaurant or waiting in a doctor's office. I wonder if we have forgotten a very important element of Godly character. What is it? It is patience, which the Oxford English Dictionary defines as, *the capacity to accept or tolerate delay, trouble, or suffering without getting angry or upset.*

In Acts, chapter 7, we are reminded of the story of Moses. At one point Moses killed an Egyptian who was mistreating an Israelite. Moses fled the country and lived in the land of Midian. Now…watch verse 30. Here's the first sentence:

> Forty years later, in the desert near Mount Sinai, an angel appeared to Moses in the flame of a burning bush.

Most of us focus on that miracle in the burning bush but miss the first part of the sentence. Moses waited forty years between the time he left Egypt to the time we next learn of God speaking to him. Don't you just wonder if Moses questioned for those forty years whether God would ever use him after killing the Egyptian? There was nothing instant in this for Moses. Even after his experience with the burning bush and being placed in leadership of the Israelites, Moses wandered in the wilderness with his people for another forty years.

Eighty years waiting upon God had to be a refining time for Moses to develop patience. There is no mention in scripture that Moses tried to hurry God along during these eighty years. Moses simply did what God asked him to do. No pushing, no complaining, just dealing with the issues in life as they came up. Moses had patience that comes only through trusting God.

So what does this mean for us today? Let's take some time and simply trust God and by doing so develop patience. Let's stop pushing God, begging for an instant answer to our prayers and understand that God doesn't reveal all things to us instantly. We don't need to always be in control. Relax and allow God to develop more patience in you. You will become a better spouse, employee, church member, friend, and community member. Enjoy your relationship with God as a home cooked meal...not as a bowl of instant soup.

# Developing Godly Character:
# The Trait of Integrity

Have you ever thought about what it means to have Godly character? What are those characteristics that God expects us to posses as His followers? Today let's talk about one of those characteristics...integrity. Most of us would simply call this honesty.

Let us look at Acts, chapter 5 verses 1-11, the story of Ananias and Sapphira. For those of you that aren't familiar with the story, Ananias decided to lie to God. He sold a piece of land, brought part of the money to the disciples, and claimed it was the full amount from the land sale. Peter confronted Ananias on his lie and said this to Ananias:

> How could you do a thing like this? You weren't lying to us but to God (Acts 5:4).

Now here is the next sentence from this passage in the Bible:

> As soon as Ananias heard these words, he fell to the floor and died (Acts 5:5).

Each of us should immediately realize the importance of not lying to God. Was there a warning not to do it again? No. Was there a small punishment? No. Did Ananias stop to explain his position on the issue? No. Ananias instantly *fell to the floor and died*.

If you don't yet understand the severity of lying to God, take a look at subsequent verses dealing with the wife of Ananias.

Peter confronted Sapphira about her part in the lie concerning the sale of this land. Peter said:

> How could the two of you even think of conspiring to test the Spirit of the Lord? The young men who buried your husband are just outside the door and they will carry you out, too (Acts 5:9).

What's the next line in the Bible? Here it is, *Instantly, she fell to the floor and died* (Acts 5:10).

How many times have you heard people say something like this: God, if you will just get me out of this situation I promise I will (fill in the blank). Let me say that each of us needs to be very careful about promises made to God and to others. Ananias and Sapphira paid with their lives for lying to God. God clearly expects integrity and honesty from his followers.

Let me challenge each of you today. When you make a promise it is just that…a promise. Situations don't change your promise, people don't change your promise, circumstances don't change your promise. Honor God and be a person of your word.

# Discarded Truth

More and more I find myself thinking about truth...truth in the form of promises. Truth that really is just that...something you can always count on. In our culture, we seldom see a promise actually kept. People hedge their words with phrases such as *I'll try*, not *I will*. Even when fixing problems, some folks say *that should work* rather than *that will work*. People break social commitments when they have a better offer from someone else or another party just seems like more fun. It's just hard to get people to keep their promises.

While I was driving through Florida, an interesting sign caught my attention. Here's what the sign said, *Uncontested divorce just $199*. I couldn't help but wonder how many of those seeking an uncontested divorce had started their marriage with a promise to God and to each other to stay together until separated by death. Now, for $199 dollars, the promise is dissolved.

I recently watched a father try to get his one-year-old son to come back to him. The energetic boy had run off to play and the father wanted him to return. This dad pretended to have candy in his hand and held his hand out to the boy asking him if he wanted some candy. The boy ran back to his dad. The dad opened his hand showing the little boy no candy and said, *Son, candy will be the death of you* and just laughed. What a lesson to teach our children to get what you want through deception and lying.

I think back to promises in the Bible and begin to understand why many folks just can't believe these promises. They have come from a world where truth is difficult to find. Promises don't have meaning. Deception and trickery are common. May I remind you that there are absolute truths that God has revealed in the Bible? These promises of God are always true.

Don't let a world of false promises keep you from believing in the truths of God. Promises from today's culture don't in any way correspond to the promises of an eternal God. Do you want to discover some of these absolute truths? Go pick up your Bible and start reading. You won't find $199 uncontested divorces there. You won't find a God who manipulates there. Instead you will find truths that you can count on all the time. Not just things that *should work* in your life but rather you will find truths that *will work* in your life, if you choose to follow God. There is no hedging when it comes to Biblical truth.

So get your Bible and start discovering absolute truth and stop relying on the promises of the world. Like the little boy, if you follow promises of the world, you will only be running after candy that doesn't exist.

# The Consumer Mindset

I was sitting with my daughter when she picked up a magazine that came to her in the mail. The magazine advertised a popular doll and a variety of doll accessories. As we looked through the magazine we started closely examining some of these doll accessories. Here are a few accessories that stood out to us from the magazine:

A science lab set ($36)

A school backpack set for dolls ($28)

Braces and retainer called the healthy smile set ($14)

Allergy free lunch for your doll ($28)

Now there are pages of accessories like this. But as my daughter and I started talking about this we couldn't help but wonder about spending priorities. Why would anyone spend this kind of money on doll accessories when we have children throughout the world that can't afford to eat? How can some people justify paying $28 for an allergy free doll lunch that will never be consumed when real children are starving? There are many reputable organizations that can feed a child for an entire month for $28.

As we think about the elements of Godly character, I can't help but believe that service to others must be on the list. In my former days as a police officer, I think about kids who had little food, those who were abused, those who only dreamed about clean clothes and a clean room, and those who desperately needed a home. I can't help but think about Matthew 10:42 that says:

And if you give even a cup of cold water to one of the least of my followers, you will surely be rewarded.

Certainly many children in our world need a cup of cold water and much more.

So instead of spending our money on things of this world with no eternal significance, instead of getting caught up in the advertising of the day, may I suggest something different? Serve those who really need your help. Offer your own cup of water and more *to one of the least of these*. Step up and make a difference in the life of a child or in the life of someone that only you can reach. Those that need help are all around us. All we need to do is look.

# The Power of *Domini Sumus*

Recently I was listening to my pastor Dr. Scott Borderud from our local Christian and Missionary Alliance church. During part of his message he used a phrase that caught my attention. Here is the phrase: *Domini Sumus*. This is a Latin phrase that simply means, *we belong to the Lord*.

Now before you start thinking those words really aren't so special, stop and think again. We belong to the Lord. This phrase is based upon Romans 14:7-8. Here is what those verses say:

> For we don't live for ourselves or die for ourselves. If we live, it's to honor the Lord. And if we die, it's to honor the Lord. So whether we live or die, we belong to the Lord.

I don't know about you but these verses provide tremendous relief for me. In the good times and the bad I belong to the Lord. When I'm having health issues, I belong to the Lord. When I have financial problems, I belong to the Lord. When I have problems at work, I belong to the Lord. I don't need to worry because in every situation, I belong to the Lord.

How about you? Are you struggling with something in your life that seems insurmountable? Something that seems overwhelming to you? Maybe you just can't see a way out and you are ready to give up. Here's some good news…if you are a follower of Christ you belong to the Lord. Don't be discouraged or give up. You are part of God's family.

So take the phrase *domini sumus* and write it on your wall, your screen saver, your to do list, your phone, or where ever you will constantly see it. Every time you look at that phrase say to yourself, *I belong to the Lord*. Take comfort in the fact that you have a heavenly Father who loves you dearly and will lead and comfort you throughout your life.

*Domini Sumus!*

# Are You Living a Dream or Chasing One?

One of the great things about my job is the opportunity I have to listen to people talk about their life dreams. I had the opportunity to listen to a very special man talk about his life dream. As this ninety-two year old man described his dream, I found myself catching the passion and the excitement he felt. You see, I quickly learned that he had spent his life not chasing his dream but rather living his dream.

So what is your life's dream? Will you accomplish it? Are you living your dream or simply chasing one?

Please understand that life dreams are very important. They give us focus, energy, and purpose. The great part about life dreams is that you get to pick your dream and design the path to accomplish it.

One of the wonderful aspects of education is that it gives students a chance to dream...to discover what they want to do with their lives. But sometimes, many of us get so bogged down in the daily details of life that our dreams get put on a shelf. Sometimes others tell us we will never accomplish our dreams so we voluntarily put them on the shelf and out of sight. John Barrymore once said:

> A man is not old until regrets take the place of dreams ("AZQuotes.com").

Have regrets replaced your dreams?

If they have, there is still hope. God gives us tremendous guidance when we choose to pursue our dreams. In the first chapter of the book of Joshua, God tells Joshua:

Be strong and courageous. Do not be afraid or dismayed for the Lord your God is with you wherever you go (Joshua 1:9).

That same promise applies to us as believers in Christ. So, take your dreams off the shelf, dust them off and remember...*be strong and courageous*. My ninety-two year old friend would look you in the eye and tell you to go dream, follow scripture, and change your life!

# Go Ahead…Drop It

Each season of the year is very special to me. Fall, winter, spring, and summer…they all have their own unique beauty. However, during the fall, I really enjoy watching the leaves change to beautiful colors. It's a special time.

Do you ever just sit and look out your window? Well, during one particular day this fall I was doing just that. I noticed leaves falling everywhere. I started to wonder about my life. Fall seems like a good time of year to intentionally drop some of my emotional leaves. How about you? Do you have some leaves to drop? Leaves of worry, leaves of sadness, leaves of hatred, leaves of indifference, leaves of selfishness, leaves of self-pity, leaves of arrogance, leaves of disappointment…is it just time to really shake your tree and get rid of those dead leaves?

Wouldn't it be wonderful for all of us to move into the future with some of our burdens released and on the ground instead of weights on our shoulders?

I hope you realize that dropping your burdens is really possible and can be a reality in your life. Psalm 55:22 says:

> Give your burdens to the LORD, and he will take care of you. He will not permit the godly to slip and fall.

You see burdens that you have been living with just make you tired. It's like carrying a weight around all the time. They are always with you and it's time to get rid of these weights.

Matthew 11:28 says this:

Then Jesus said, Come to me, all of you who are weary and carry heavy burdens, and I will give you rest.

So, now is your chance. Take a lesson from the trees in your own yard and drop those dead leaves that have been weighing you down. Throw them off, release the weight, and give them to Jesus. Then you will really experience the rest that comes in Christ.

# Failing with Class

I was talking with a man that told me the incredible story of his work history. This man is clearly an entrepreneur and is wired to be creative. At one point in his life, he landed his dream job. He was the president of a company; he was having fun at work, making a lot of money, and really enjoying life.

In the blink of an eye, he found himself without a job, no income, bills to pay, and a family to support. He felt like a failure. He had messed up everything. What would you do if that happened to you? You see, what you do with failure shows your true character. What you do when you fail determines the kind of person you are and who you will become. Here are some things to consider when you fail:

First, understand that at some point in your life you will fail at something. If you are anything like me you will have multiple failures in life. So get ready and think about how you will handle failure. As a friend of mine often says:

Life is full of failures so buy a helmet.

In other words, understand failure is part of life and prepare for it.

Second, what lessons can you learn from failure? When you do fail, stop and examine what happened. As John Maxwell says, you don't get knocked to the floor very often but while you're down there, clean up something. Figure out what went wrong and learn from it (Maxwell, *Failing*).

Third, don't let failure cause you to fear the future. Remember the man I spoke about earlier? He took his failure, learned some lessons, cleaned up some things while he was down on the floor, and is now the president of his own company…doing what he loves and enjoying a wonderful life. Failure didn't scare him; it challenged him to push harder.

So, when failure happens, learn from your mistakes, get out your mop and clean up some things while you are knocked down, and ask God to give you strength to stand up and charge ahead.

In Psalm 18:32 we read: *God arms me with strength, and He makes my way perfect*. So take God at his word. Not only will he provide strength during times of failure but He will help you get back on track.

# Finish the Race Well

Have you ever watched videos of people involved in a race when things didn't work out as planned? I'm talking about track, cross-country, or Olympic races where folks just struggled to finish the race. The winner may have crossed far ahead but these stragglers crossed the finish line limping, crawling, or leaning on someone else.

What intrigues me about individual races like these is that I find myself always rooting for these folks who just won't give up. I keep hoping they will just go a little farther and keep trying so they can eventually finish the race. I somehow think that many of you feel as I do and find yourself cheering for these underdogs. We find ourselves celebrating the winner of the race but rejoicing for the ones who struggled but finally completed the race. We just want to celebrate the one who would not quit. We often admire those who struggle and finish more than those who coast to an easy victory.

Sometimes in our lives we become so focused on winning our spiritual race that we forget it is more important to finish the race. The race I'm talking about here is our life-long relationship with Christ, honoring scripture, and spreading the gospel. If we would be honest with ourselves we would know that we are not just going to coast through life with few problems, never questioning what God is teaching us, and free of difficult times. Life is tough…spiritual races are tough. In our spiritual race we might find ourselves limping to the finish but we must finish strong.

When I think of a spiritual race I think of 2 Timothy 4:7. Here is what this scripture says:

> I have fought the good fight, I have finished the race, and I have remained faithful.

So...how are you doing in your spiritual race? Are you remaining faithful to the cause of Christ? Are you helping others get to the finish line? Are you running a good race or are you out of breath, hunched over, and stopped along the side of the track? Maybe you even feel like giving up.

Well, I have good news for you today. If you find that you are like one of those athletes trying to get to the finish line of your spiritual race but you seem to be on your hands and knees crawling your way to the finish line, I want you to remember that we have a God who is able to lift you up and support you in your race. No matter your circumstances, you are not running alone. Don't give up! Put your trust in God to see you through to the finish line of your spiritual race.

# FOMO

This week, I was reading about researchers who study folks that just can't seem to put down their electronic devices. You know the people I'm talking about…those who just can't stay off Facebook, are constantly checking their phones for the latest text message, or just can't stop watching their email. We see them at restaurants checking their electronic devices while they eat. We see them walking down the street paying little attention to traffic as they check their devices. In fact, I recently watched a video of a woman sending a text message as she walked right off an ocean pier into the water.

Researchers now have even given this behavior a name. They call it FOMO, which stands for *fear of missing out*. Several researchers believe that some people are so afraid that they are missing something important that they just can't put down their electronic devices for fear of missing out. They can't stand the thought that they might miss out on the latest Facebook status, miss a text, or might miss that important work email.

When is the last time you had spiritual FOMO? When is the last time you had a fear of missing out on something that God had just for you? Are you so busy running from appointment to appointment that you don't even have time to think about God's plans for you? Can you even remember the last time you asked God what he has in store for you?

It's not a surprise to God that our human nature keeps pushing us to do more…often occupying ourselves with tasks that have nothing to do with eternity. In Psalm 46:10 God says:

Be still and know that I am God.

You see God knows sometimes we just need to disengage and *be still* in the presence of God. It is in those moments we can listen to God and make certain that we aren't missing out on what He has for each of us.

Disengage from your daily routine and simply be still in the presence of God. Ask God if you are missing out on something that He has in store for you. You may just receive the best gift you can imagine.

# Found Letters

According to KXTV in California, Chuck Kunellis was surprised this month when two letters his father wrote to his wife almost seventy years ago were finally delivered to Chuck's home. Chuck's father wrote the letters while stationed in Italy during World War II. The letters had been lost in the mail and, through the work of a Good Samaritan, were finally delivered to Chuck (Clarke).

Whatever your situation with your earthly father, you always have letters that are available to you from your heavenly Father. Simply stated, those letters are found in the Bible. God knew that throughout time all of us would need letters of encouragement, direction, and love. Scripture provides us with God's ageless, remarkable letters. Are you feeling discouraged? Read Psalms. Looking for direction? Read Proverbs? Looking for love? Go to the book of John and learn just how much God really loves you.

In an article from Christianity today, LifeWay Research surveyed more than 2,900 Protestant churchgoers and found that while ninety percent of those surveyed *desire to please and honor Jesus in all they do,* only nineteen percent personally read the Bible every day (Rankin).

How about you? How are you doing with the letters from your heavenly Father? Are you reading them daily? If you're struggling with your Bible reading, just remember that reading God's word is not an obligation. It's not a chore that you must complete and cross off your list. Your reading is a chance to learn more about God. It's a chance to hear Him speak to you through his letters. Deuteronomy 7:9 tells us:

> Understand, therefore, that the Lord your God is indeed God. He is the faithful God who keeps his covenant for a thousand generations and lavishes his unfailing love on those who love him and obey his commandments.

Keep reading your Bible and see what God has written just for you. It would be a shame to leave a letter from God unopened.

# The Fourth Trimester

Let's talk about fourth trimester abortions. I hope you are already asking yourself what this means. The term itself makes no sense. By definition a trimester has three parts, not four. Dan Joseph, in his video, explained that his made up term of *fourth trimester abortion* would allow the killing of an infant after birth. Dan visited the campus of George Mason University armed with his fictitious petition seeking signatures to support fourth trimester abortions. Within one hour Dan obtained fourteen signatures on his petition.

Dan went to George Mason armed with his petition and gave the usual pro-choice rhetoric as students passed by. Few students asked about the definition of a fourth trimester abortion and many simply signed the petition.

One student asked if this procedure would harm the baby! After learning that it would she signed anyway. Frankly, I don't know what part of the definition of abortion she didn't understand. Abortion ends a pregnancy and ends a life. Why would you even ask if this harms the baby? A second student is told not to even read the petition just to sign it and without any consideration for the content of the petition signs his name.

What are some lessons here? First, if this is the best that our higher education system can provide in terms of critical thinking skills we have a serious problem. Not all colleges and universities are created equal. Even a faculty member at this particular college signed the petition.

Go find a college that provides some critical thinking skills and stop wasting your money on colleges that leave you agreeing with fourth trimester abortions and unable to discern between truth and fiction. Better still; don't go to any college that leaves you supporting abortion as a viable alternative. Develop some critical thinking skills and you will soon see the fallacies in the pro-choice agenda. Former President Ronald Reagan understood the weakness in the pro-choice arguments when he said:

> I've noticed that everyone who is for abortion has already been born (Wooly).

Second, don't put a lot of credibility in petitions. People will sign almost anything. Next time you hear about a petition with 100,000 names on it just remember these fourteen clueless folks who supported fourth trimester abortions.

Finally, don't forget the wisdom found in the Bible. The book of Proverbs warns us about our need for wisdom and says this:

> Wisdom shouts in the streets. She cries out in the public square. She calls to the crowds along the main street, to those gathered in front of the city gate: How long, you simpletons, will you insist on being simpleminded? How long will you mockers relish your mocking? How long will you fools hate knowledge? Come and listen to my counsel. I'll share my heart with you and make you wise (Proverbs 1:20-33).

Wisdom is calling to each of us. It's time to start listening.

# A Concert to Remember

It seems someone is always telling us to count our blessings…to remember all those things for which we should be thankful. While this is great advice, sometimes we only think about things to be grateful about rather than developing an attitude of gratefulness.

I was reading about a lady who attended a Garth Brooks concert. During the concert Garth was singing a very popular song he wrote called *The Dance*. As he was singing this song, a lady from the audience held up a sign that read:

Chemo this morning

Garth tonight

Enjoying the dance (Sunny)

Let's stop for a moment and think about this sign and what it signals about attitude. I have been around many people who I simply call an *energy leak* (Jones). When they talk to you the joy of life seems to just get pulled from your body. You can feel these folks draining the energy right out of you! These energy leaks complain over trivial matters and the complaining seems endless. Every time you try to get away they take you by the arm and complain some more.

Contrast this with the woman holding the sign. If anyone has something to complain about it's this woman. Suffering from cancer and chemotherapy she makes a choice to be thankful. She could choose to sit at home and complain but instead she decides to go celebrate life at a Garth Brooks concert (Jones).

You see our decision to be thankful for what we have is a choice. We can choose to be an energy leak...a drain on others...or we can choose to be a light to the world...showing the world what it really means to be a follower of Christ.

I am reminded of this verse in Psalm 118:24 that says:

> This is the day that the Lord has made; let us rejoice and be glad in it.

This is a short but powerful verse. In all we do, each and every day choose to rejoice!

Remember to focus on a thankful attitude like the woman with the sign. Your attitude really is a choice and God, through His word, has told us the right choice to make. It's simple...be thankful and rejoice.

# Knowing God's Will for You

Do you ever wonder how to know God's will for your life? I think most of us deal with this. I certainly can't speak to what God's plan is for your life but let me give you a few thoughts to consider when you're facing tough decisions. I find these three considerations helpful when I have searched for God's direction.

First, is the decision you are considering scriptural? If you are considering something that the Bible clearly warns against, stay away from it.

Second, do you have the skills for what you are considering? I realize you won't have all the skills necessary for moving in a new direction (and frankly you shouldn't) but are you wired for the new opportunity you are considering? If you are wired to be a visionary person and the opportunity you are considering has you doing detailed work every day it might not be the right fit.

Third, do you need to force things to make the new opportunity happen? I have seen so many folks try to manipulate or force situations to get what they desire. I think of one person I know who has tried to become a college president for fifteen years, forcing her way through every possible opportunity. It still hasn't happened and she continues dealing with frustration. She has probably missed out on other wonderful job opportunities throughout the fifteen years. Don't be afraid to take your hands off and let God open the doors.

I look for all three of these criteria to line up. I look for three green lights. If everything lines up, I start to walk through the doors. Remember, doors can close, but these three standards have always helped me determine if I should start walking through the open doors.

# God's Rescue Squad

Summer is a big time for churches all across America to host vacation bible school. One church in Carthage, MO did just that. In fact, they called their bible school program *God's Rescue Squad*. Each day of the week the church invited different rescue squads to come visit the church and show the kids what rescue squads really do. The paramedics came on Monday, the fire department on Tuesday, the Jasper County Sheriff's Department brought their K-9 unit out on Wednesday. On Thursday the church wanted to honor the National Guard. Guess who refused to come? You guessed it...the National Guard.

The church was told it was against military policy for the National Guard to participate in any church vacation bible school program. Here's how the National Guard policy reads:

> Army participation must not selectively benefit (or appear to benefit) any person, group, or corporation (whether profit or nonprofit); religion, sect, religious or sectarian group, or quasi-religious or ideological movement (Starnes "Military").

Here are two quotes from the members of the National Guard who were not permitted to attend the vacation bible school:

> I can tell you I'm ashamed and embarrassed right now. This isn't the military I signed up for (Starnes "Military").

How about this comment from another National Guard member:

> We had a lot of disappointed kiddos because of the National Guard being unwilling to allow a Humvee and a few soldiers to spend an hour at a Baptist church. It

makes me wonder what I'm actually fighting for (Starnes "Military").

But wait...let's back up the bus a minute. Look at the policy we just noted: *Army participation must not selectively benefit...any person, group, etc.*

In June of 2014, our military color guard marched in the 39th Annual Capital Pride parade...which specifically celebrates the gay agenda. The Washington D.C. Color Guard began the parade immediately following a motorcycle group called Dykes on Bikes. This is the same color guard that presents official colors for the President of the United States, members of Congress, and countless official state functions (librarisingnsf).

This very military policy, so concerned with showing favoritism to a specific group and preventing our soldiers from showing Humvees to six year olds at a church vacation bible school does not prevent our soldiers from marching in a gay pride parade. I always thought policies applied to everyone. Apparently in the military they do not.

If the military (or anyone else) is going to give certain groups preferential treatment, I wish they would just tell us. How about some honesty? I sure get tired of the political spin. Just tell the truth. We would all feel better about you.

# A Hymn That Hit Home

I was in Florida completing some work for Toccoa Falls College. It had been a busy couple of days and I had a lot on my mind. I was trying to resolve quite a few issues, checking on college finances as we quickly approached the end of the fiscal year, and finalizing plans for graduation...my head was swirling with things I needed to complete.

On this particular day, I was attending a luncheon and sat down at my table thinking about all these different things while getting ready to speak to the group attending the luncheon. The Toccoa Falls College choir was at this luncheon event and started to sing. They sang a very familiar song called *Great Is Thy Faithfulness*. Many of you are very familiar with this old hymn of the church.

In 1925, Thomas Chisholm wrote this wonderful song. Chisholm led what many of us would call a very ordinary life. He was born in a log cabin in Kentucky. He entered the ministry at age 36 but retired after just one year because of poor health. Chisholm spent the rest of his life working as a life insurance salesman. But even with his desk job he wrote almost 1,200 poems and published several hymns. Here is what Chisholm said toward the end of his life:

> My income has not been large at any time due to impaired health in the earlier years which has followed me on until now. Although I must not fail to record here the unfailing faithfulness of a covenant-keeping God and that He has given me many wonderful displays of His providing care,

for which I am filled with astonishing gratefulness (Gathers).

So hearing the Toccoa Falls College choir sing this wonderful hymn, I found myself remembering that God is always faithful. I again remembered that I don't need to do everything myself. God has been unbelievably faithful throughout my life. I am reminded of these lines from the hymn:

> Pardon for Sin and a peace that endureth,
> Thine own dear presence to cheer and to guide,
> Strength for today and bright hope for tomorrow
> Blessings all mine, with ten thousand beside!

So, next time you start to get overwhelmed with the daily pressures of life, just remember the wonderful faithfulness of our God. As a follower of Christ, He has always been there for you and always will see you through whatever you are facing.

# I Think I Am in Control

Do you ever have days when you feel as though everything is spinning out of control? Just that very thought implies that you actually believe you control your days. Could it be that we often forget who actually controls each day?

I think it is very common for those who are driven and goal oriented to fall into the trap of believing that we can force things to happen. If we push hard enough we can make events occur. We believe that we control our days, our careers, and even our futures. We have the latest computer calendars, to do lists, project management software, strategic plans, and we read the latest books on organizing and managing our lives, families, and co-workers.

Maybe we need to just stop and take a breath and reflect on what scripture tells us. In Proverbs 16:9, we read:

We can make our plans but the Lord determines our steps.

I believe a great partner verse to this is found in Psalms 46:10. Here we read:

Be still, and know that I am God.

Be still…now there is something to think about. My days are filled with endless pinging…the indication of new email arriving, text messages, Twitter notifications, my cell phone ringing. How do I ever hear God directing my steps? It's that verse in Psalms…reminding me to sit down, calm down, relax, and *be still*. As I obey I begin to hear God speaking to me.

So…if God is in control, how can your life be out of control? If you have turned your life over to Christ, it is impossible for your life to be out of control. Turn your life over to God, listen to His direction, and relax. God has determined your steps.

# We Didn't Really Need
# Those Books Anyway

Todd Starnes from Fox News recently reported on a charter school in California that decided to purge books...not just any books though. According to this report, the school decided to remove all books from their library that were *written by a Christian author or had a Christian message*. Nothing like a library that tells you what you are going to read.

A parent who happened to be visiting the school discovered this book purging. According to the Pacific Justice Institute who is helping correct this issue, a parent of one of the students was told:

> ...the library would no longer be carrying those [Christian] books (Starnes, "Atty").

In fact, the Pacific Justice Institute reported that their client actually took some of the Christian books from the library after the library decided to give the books away.

According to the report, one of the books that was purged from the school library was a book titled, *The Hiding Place* written by Corrie ten Boom. Ten Boom was a Christian who actually prevented many Jews from being sent to Nazi concentration camps and saved countless lives.

When questioned about this purging, the school superintendent said this:

> We are a public school, and as such, we are barred by law from purchasing sectarian curriculum materials with state

funds. We only keep on our shelves the books that we are authorized to purchase with public funds (Starnes, "Atty").

So, now it really gets interesting. Who decides what is sectarian curriculum. Todd Starnes makes an interesting point here. He asks what about the work of the Rev. Dr. Martin Luther King Jr.? Should that be purged? After all, he is a pastor. Should all his writing about the civil rights movement be purged because he has *Rev.* in front of his name?

And why should any library purge material in the first place? What a way to silence those who disagree with your beliefs...just remove all the opposition's writing from your shelves. Let's not engage in open dialog about differing points of view; let's just remove the arguments from our library shelves.

I always thought educational institutions were places for open debate and discussion. I suppose when you believe the light of truth will expose the errors of your beliefs, it's just easier to win the debate by silencing your critics.

# Forget Common Sense

InterVarsity Christian Fellowship (IVCF) is a wonderful organization that has been telling college students about the power of the gospel for more than seven decades. They can be found on 616 college campuses and have 949 chapters serving college students.

For years, IVCF has been a part of campuses associated with the California State University system (CSU). IVCF has 23 chapters on 19 CSU campus locations. Until now.

California State University system implemented a new nondiscrimination policy. As part of this policy, CSU no longer recognizes InterVarsity Christian Fellowship as an official student organization.

Why this change? Because IVCF will not allow students to lead their chapters if they do not agree with basic, historic Christian beliefs. The CSU system now requires that all their student groups accept all students, regardless of their beliefs, as group leaders.

Here is what a representative from IVCF said about this new policy:

> While InterVarsity invites and welcomes all students as participants, we believe a Christian group should have the right to expect and even require their leaders to be Christian – just as any student group, club or Greek organization should be able to require their leaders to be like minded (Murashko).

Before you begin to think that the IVCF is a closed group and CSU needed to take action to make them more inclusive, approximately 50% of students active in IVCF are members of ethnic minority groups, in California the number is closer to 70%.

Why should any organization be forced to allow someone to lead them who doesn't believe in what the organization believes? Would a church hire a pastor who disagreed with the beliefs of the church? Would the military keep a general who didn't believe in the constitution? Would a Chinese restaurant hire a manager who knows nothing about Chinese food? Of course not. Yet, we are telling a Christian group they must be willing to be led by those who don't even believe in Christianity.

For a university, like the California State University, who should be leading others in critical thinking skills, this decision to remove IVCF from their campuses is inexcusable. Yet again, in our politically correct world, common sense, rest in peace.

# The Concept of Intelligent Design

I have always been intrigued with the study of intelligent design. If you're not familiar with this scientific area of study, one dictionary defines intelligent design as the theory that life, or the universe, cannot have developed by chance but was designed and created by some intelligent entity. In other words, creation and even the human body show such complexity in design that the chances of forming through some type of random process are mathematically improbable. These design complexities point to an intelligent creator. Many of us believe that creator is the God of the Bible.

Dr. Stephen Meyer is a well-known researcher in the area of intelligent design. He has scientifically evaluated many aspects of creation including the chance that DNA contained in our body could simply form randomly. As Dr. Meyer points out, the creation of DNA in the body is a three-step process. First, an amino acid strand is necessary for the formulation of DNA. What are the chances of just a small strand of amino acids forming randomly? Dr. Meyer calculated the chance of this occurring randomly as one chance in $10^{30}$. That is the number 1 with 30 zeros after it! Second, every amino acid must have a mirror of itself to function properly. What are the chances of random mirroring of the amino acid? Dr. Meyer calculates this as one in $10^{60}$. Finally, Dr. Meyer tells us that the strands must be in a specific sequence. He explains they must be arranged like letters in a sentence to make sense. What are the chances of this happening randomly? Dr. Meyer has calculated this chance as one in $10^{130}$ (Klinghoffer).

This week CNN published an article called, *Are We Born With a Moral Core? The Baby Lab Says Yes*. This Yale University study attempted to answer the following question:

> Are we born knowing the difference between good and evil or are these moral beliefs taught (Chun)?

This article notes that many researchers now believe that babies are born with a sense of morality…that parents and society can help develop this morality but that neither parents nor society can create the actual belief system. The understanding of good and evil is already built into us at birth. Could an intelligent designer have built that into each of us? A lot of scientific evidence is pointing in that direction.

So the team at Yale University is telling us that babies are born with an understanding of good and evil…evidence that a Creator placed that within each of us. Dr. Stephen Meyer is doing remarkable work using science to show an intelligent designer in both the creation of the universe and our very bodies. Again, showing us that the chances of humans randomly developing are mathematically almost impossible.

Scientific evidence clearly points to an intelligent designer. Maybe it is time for us to realize there is a wonderful Creator who cares about us and has made us all in a wonderful way. Perhaps we all need to realize that all truth is God's truth and that includes the truth in scientific studies that points to a creator. You are not alone in this world. God created you and the world you live in. Stay open to what God has planned for you.

# Is the Bible True?

If someone asked you to explain how you know the Bible is true, what would you say? Would you be at a loss for words? Would your brain just be whirling trying to come up with some logical response? For many of us the answer to both of these questions would be *yes*.

I was talking with a man who was asked this very question: *How do you know the Bible is true?* His response? *Because God said it is true.* Now, OK, those of us brought up in the church sort of get that answer. However, if you don't believe in God to begin with, that answer won't get you very far. In our culture, the decision to believe in God is often directly linked to whether the person can believe in God's word...the Bible.

There is a specific field of study in Christian theology called apologetics. Apologetics is a branch of Christian theology devoted to the intellectual defense of faith (Merriam-Webster).

Each of us needs to clearly understand the major arguments used by today's culture that attempt to defeat the validity of scripture. Many of the common arguments are the same and simply passed on from person to person. Arguments such as discrepancies in scripture, problems with translations of the original texts, the Bible is too old, etc. With a little study you can easily talk about these topics with unbelievers and answer many of these objections to scripture.

Studying some apologetics isn't simply a nice thing to do. God requires it. In I Peter 3:15 we are told:

...you must worship Christ as Lord of your life. And if someone asks about your Christian hope, always be ready to explain it.

So are you ready to explain your Christian hope? If you're not, here is a quick way to get started. Lee Strobel wrote three books that will get you well on your way to discovering answers to confirm the truth of the Bible. Strobel was an atheist working for the Chicago Tribune as an investigative reporter. He holds a Master of Studies in Law degree from Yale Law School and a journalism degree from the University of Missouri. After investigating the evidence for Christ he became a follower of Christ and has documented the evidence pointing toward the truth of scripture (Strobel).

So get started on your mini apologetics journey and pick up three of Strobel's books. First, read *The Case for Christ*. Second, read *The Case for Faith*, and finally pick up *The Case for the Resurrection*. You will be amazed at what you find and I promise you that your faith in the truth of scripture will be bolstered as you read these books.

Here's a warning. Be careful. Apologetic studies can be habit forming but one thing is certain. After a little study, you will certainly be able to clearly explain your Christian hope.

# It's Not About You

Have you ever heard statements like this?

I was here first.

I have my rights.

You owe me.

Can't you move any faster?

We live in a society today where many folks just believe life is all about them. If they don't get what they want they complain loudly. If they are served a bit too slowly at a restaurant they are quick to lean over to your table and tell you about it. If they believe their rights have been violated they will quickly take legal action.

I can't help but think about the scripture in Matthew, chapter 20, verse 26 that says:

> Whoever wants to be a leader among you must be your servant, and whoever wants to be first among you must become your slave. For even the Son of Man came not to be served but to serve others and to give his life as a ransom for many.

Are you serving others or are you waiting to be served? Is it all about you or is it about making a Godly impact in the lives of others? By simply examining the life of Christ we can easily understand what He meant in those verses from Matthew. Jesus spent a lifetime helping those around Him. He healed the sick, fed the hungry, raised the dead, loved the poor, taught the children, and ultimately died a terrible death on a cross for all of us.

So next time you encounter the sales clerk having a tough day or the waiter or waitress just at the end of their rope, remember it's not about us. Show them an extra measure of kindness that they just don't expect. Show them the kindness of a loving God who came to serve. Show them what having God in your life is all about.

# Kindness Matters

I was reading a sign the other day that had a very simple message. Here it is...*kindness matters*. What could be simpler? Yet we live in a world where many folks are self-absorbed. The world revolves around them and there just isn't time for anyone else.

While I was traveling I noticed a couple who appeared to be in their eighties. They were enjoying dinner in a restaurant a few tables over from me. A man who had been eating at another table walked over to this older couple's table and simply asked how long they had been married. It turned out the older couple had been married over sixty years. The older man was a veteran and told the other man of battles he had been in and how he loves America. The entire conversation took about five minutes. The younger man told the couple how much he appreciated the older man's service to our country and the fact that he and his wife had stayed married through good times and bad.

Then the younger man did something really special. He took the bill for the older couple's dinner and told them dinner was on him. The older couple looked shocked and I could clearly see tears start to well up in the older man's eyes. The younger man shook their hands and was off. I never heard any of them exchange names and I'm certain they will never see each other again.

When is the last time you went out on a limb and put your Christian beliefs into practice expecting nothing in return? The book of Proverbs in chapter 3, verse 3, tells us:

Never let loyalty and kindness leave you! Tie them around your neck as a reminder. Write them deep within your heart.

So follow the advice of Proverbs and that simple sign I talked about earlier. Kindness matters...never let it leave you. But don't forget, it's not enough to believe that. Take some time and put it into action whenever you can. Look for opportunities. They are all around us.

# The Power of Laughter

I enjoy having lunch with our college students. Over a recent lunch with students they had me laughing so hard my face ached. Think back to some of the times you laughed so hard you could barely stand up or you laughed so hard that you began to cry tears of joy. During those times didn't your problems begin to melt away? Didn't you begin to see your serious life issues in a different perspective? Those things you were so concerned about suddenly became lighter and easier to bear.

Many studies today show that laughter has many of the same health benefits as exercise. Other studies show that laughter has brain-boosting powers. If laughter can improve the health and mental condition of folks, I suspect we all know people who need to laugh more.

One study from Loma Linda University found that laughter raised levels of disease-fighting mechanisms in your body and increased learning ability (Bains).

Another study by a cardiologist from the University of Maryland Medical Center in Baltimore found that laughter has numerous health benefits including pain reduction, strengthening of the immune system, increase in lung volume, increased oxygenation of the blood, and reduction of the stress hormone, cortisol (Chindamo).

Surprised? As followers of Christ we shouldn't be. The Bible gave us this same information long before these medical studies took place. In Proverbs 17:22, we read:

A cheerful heart is good medicine...

We all need to laugh more and enjoy life. It really is that simple.

So this week take some time to see the humor in life. Laugh with your family, friends, co-workers, church members, and those that share your life. I bet after a good belly laugh you will have an attitude change that helps keep your life problems in perspective.

Remember, *A cheerful heart is good medicine...* Come on now...you know it's true!

# Leading and Learning

We are all leaders. We have either influenced others or we will influence others. Our influence may be at work, at home, in church, or a variety of other places.

As leaders, we need to treat leadership just as we would any sport or hobby we want to develop. What we do each day to improve our leadership skills prepares us for the tough leadership decisions of tomorrow and allows us to be leaders of significance.

Basketball legend Larry Bird became an outstanding free-throw shooter by practicing 500 shots each morning before he went to school (Katzeff).

A friend of mine is a triathlete and gets a lot of recognition on race day. However, few people know that he gets up to train at four every morning. By the time most people get to work he has already put in almost half a workday just to improve his skills.

*Champions don't become champions in the ring - they are merely recognized there* (Maxwell, *The 21*). Likewise, leaders don't become leaders in critical times – they are merely recognized there. Good leaders prepare all their lives for the big game.

In chapter 3, verse 23, of the book of Colossians we are told:

> Work willingly at whatever you do, as though you were working for the Lord rather than for people.

As leaders this applies to developing our leadership skills.

You have others watching how you lead and you are influencing their decisions. Take time each day to improve your leadership skills. Sometimes we only get one chance to influence someone. So, always improve your skills, be ready, and lead!

# Letter for the Future

During some study time, I learned about the life of twelve-year-old Taylor Smith. Taylor died from complications related to pneumonia. As you might imagine, her family was devastated…a young girl full of life with no expectation of death.

However, days after Taylor's death her parents found something that showed them just how special Taylor really was. They found a letter in a sealed envelope that Taylor wrote to herself. On the envelope Taylor wrote this: *to be opened by Taylor Smith on April 13, 2023 only* (Torres).

Because of Taylor's death, her parents decided to open the letter. What they found was amazing. Taylor wrote a letter to herself to see what she had become ten years in the future. Taylor's letter talked about a variety of things but one thing she said really stands out. Talking to herself in what she thought would be 2023, Taylor wrote this:

> …how's your relationship with GOD? Have you prayed, worshipped, read the Bible, or gone to serve the Lord recently? If not, get up and do so NOW! I don't care what point in our life we're in right now, do it (Torres)!

So a twelve-year-old girl has the foresight to want to know ten years in the future how her relationship is with God. In twelve short years, Taylor had learned something about her relationship with God that many of us struggle with daily. Taylor learned that she couldn't postpone her relationship with God. It's just too important to wait. In Taylor's words, *I don't care what point in our life we're in right now, do it* (Torres)!

Let me ask you what Taylor asked herself. How's your relationship with God? Have you prayed, worshipped, read the Bible, or gone to serve the Lord recently? Our lives get so busy that sometimes we push our relationship with God to the sideline. We think we will get around to God when the time is right. We sideline God thinking there will always be time.

Let's take a lesson from a young girl whose priority was her relationship with a God she loved dearly. As Taylor would remind us, it doesn't matter where you are in your life right now. Stop and make sure God is your priority. Don't wait...do it now!

# What Is Your Life Story?

I was talking with the chief financial officer of a bank in Atlanta. As we were comparing some leadership challenges, she used a phrase that really caught my attention. She started to talk about what her *life story* would be…what her family, employees, and friends would say about her character and actions when her life comes to an end. *Life story*…those two words really do capture a remarkable concept.

You see, your life story is just that…a story of your entire life. It doesn't simply capture a particularly good moment in your life nor does it capture a single difficult time in your life. Your life story encompasses your entire life…from birth to death.

You may have had a difficult start to your life. Perhaps you have engaged in activities or actions that today you regret. Perhaps you are saddened by the way you treated friends or family. Perhaps you are living a secret, sinful life completely opposite from the life you are portraying to those around you. You see, as long as you are alive your life story continues to develop. It's not too late to have a happy ending to your story. It's not too late to create a best seller.

As we think about our own life story, it is easy to get caught up in expectations of the world. Working eighty-hour weeks for more money while ignoring our families, forgetting biblical principles when we make decisions, not taking time each day to listen to God's prompting, forgetting the importance of being a part of the local church, omitting Bible reading from you life, and the list could go on.

The Bible clearly gives us warning about our life story. In Mark, chapter 8, verse 36, we are cautioned:

> ...what do you benefit if you gain the whole world but lose your own soul.

God was clearly talking to each of us about the importance of our life story. Is your life a mess? Does your life story need some work? It's never too late. Stop what you're doing right now and ask God to give you a new life story. You might need to make some changes in your life but when it's all said and done I am confident you want a best seller for others to read and a life that is richly blessed by God.

# Listening to God

When is the last time God spoke to you? I know that question might sound a bit odd to you but shouldn't you be having regular conversations with God? This is a relationship, right? In relationships we communicate so how is your communication going with God?

People often ask me this question: *How do I know what God wants me to do?* My response is the same. I simply ask folks what they are doing to hear God speak to them?

With a world full of email, texting, Instagram, Facebook, Twitter and all the other technological ways to communicate, no wonder many of us are missing out on hearing God. We check our phone every time it dings for the latest status update but we won't spend time with God.

Even the Psalmist, David, recognized the need to spend time talking with God. Psalm 27, verse 8 says:

> My heart has heard you say, Come and talk with me. And my heart responds, Lord, I am coming.

So how do we talk with God? Psalm 46, verse 10 gives us a great place to start the conversation. Here is what this verse tells us:

> Be still and know that I am God.

Right there in that small verse is the key to the start of the conversation...*be still.* That means we need to intentionally set aside time to talk with God. That shouldn't be a surprise to us. In our earthly relationships we make time to talk with folks. We get together for coffee, lunch, holidays or a variety of reasons just to talk and be together. David tells us we should be doing the same thing to talk with God.

It is in the stillness that you can begin to hear God speak with you. It is in that time that you set aside just to develop the relationship between you and God that you will hear Him speak.

So, be like David who desired to hear God's voice and like David simply say, *Lord, I'm coming. God, I want to hear your voice.* Set aside time for the conversation and don't let anything disturb that special time. You might be surprised by what you've been missing and by what God has to say.

# Married For A Lifetime

Do you ever just get tired hearing about divorce? I sure do. We hear the statistics almost daily on how many marriages fail. We hear about the children dealing with the aftermath of a broken family. We hear about folks who say marriage just isn't for them. Some of these folks simply choose to live together to see how things work out.

Mexico is considering two-year marriage contracts. The contracts simply expire. If the marriage is going well, you can renew your contract. If not, the marriage neatly ends (Leff).

Psychology Today also had a recent article in support of term marriages. The author said: *The term marital contract with a renewal option idea holds considerable potential to create conditions for free choice, communication and negotiation* (Wexler).

Today I want to take you on a different direction and tell you about Don and Maxine Simpson. According to one of their grandchildren, after Don and Maxine were married, they became inseparable.

Don's health began to slip after he took a fall. During the same time, Maxine's cancer took a turn for the worse. Suddenly, Don and Maxine found themselves dying next to each other in separate hospital beds. But what happened next is remarkable.

One of the grandchildren taking care of Don and Maxine reported that she heard Maxine take her last breath and she was gone. Maxine was dead.

A short time later this same grandchild accompanied health care workers who removed Maxine's body from the room. Here's what the grandchild reported:

> I walked them out with her body, walked back to check on grandpa and he quit breathing as soon as her body left the room (Christie).

They had been married for sixty-two years.

This story is a word picture for the commitment we should find in marriage. This is what scripture speaks about in Mark 10:7, where we read:

> This explains why a man leaves his father and mother and is joined to his wife, and the two are united into one. Since they are no longer two but one, let no one split apart what God has joined together.

Don and Maxine had become one flesh. What God had joined nobody was going to separate. Congratulations to Don and Maxine for understanding what marriage commitment means and for modeling that to the rest of the world.

# The Meaning of Easter

Let's think about the meaning of Easter. For many in the world, Easter is simply another holiday. Many attend church on Easter but don't fully comprehend the importance of Easter to the very foundation of our Christian faith.

The Barna Group, which conducts a variety of Christian-based research, discovered this in their surveys about Easter. Here is what they said:

> While a majority of Americans indicated some type of spiritual connection with Easter, the research also showed that a minority of adults directly linked Easter to the Christian faith's belief in the resurrection of Christ. In all, 42% of Americans said that the meaning of Easter was the resurrection of Jesus or that it signifies Christ's death and return to life. One out of every 50 adults (2%) said that they would describe Easter as the most important holiday of their faith (Barna).

What about you? Do you believe that Jesus was who He said He was? There is a very telling portion of scripture in the book of John, chapter 19. At this point in scripture, Jesus was to be crucified and Pilate had ordered a sign be placed on the cross that read, *Jesus of Nazareth, the King of the Jews*. If we begin reading in verse 21 we find this:

> Then the leading priests objected and said to Pilate, Change it from 'The King of the Jews' to 'He said, I am King of the Jews.'

Now listen to Pilate's reply. Pilate said, *No, what I have written, I have written*. Let's think about this for a moment. Pilate is the

Roman ruler who has appeased the Jews by allowing the killing of Jesus but yet he won't change the sign on the cross? That is very telling. It seems that Pilate knew something the rest of us should clearly know…Jesus is the King of the Jews. Jesus is who He said He is. In I Peter 2:24, we read:

> He (Jesus) personally carried our sins in His body on the cross so that we can be dead to sin and live for what is right. By His wounds you are healed.

If you don't know Jesus, I invite you to meet Him today. By His wounds your sins are forgiven and by His wounds your broken life can be healed. The crucifixion was only the beginning of the story. The story ends with a miraculous resurrection…a God who lives. A God not impacted by the power of the grave. If the crucifixion were the end of the story there would be nothing to celebrate…there would be no point to Easter. But we do have a reason to celebrate Easter and this God can be the leader of your life if you simply allow Him to lead.

So now the choice is yours. Try to live on your own with no hope for eternity or live with the King who will bring you joy that you cannot imagine. I think Pilate knew who Jesus was and I suspect you do too. Change your life and live for the King today.

# Meeting with God

I was talking with a friend who asked me a question that stopped me in my tracks. He said this: *When was the last time you went to church and really expected to meet with God?* Sure…most of us regularly attend church but do we actually prepare for church?

I know for many families our weekly list of tasks includes attending church on Sunday. At 10:30 AM we know we must be sitting in our seat at church. We have hurried to get our children dressed, get breakfast, keep our family moving out the door and get seated but have we forgotten the most important part? Have we even thought about preparing our hearts all week for what God is going to do in that Sunday church service?

When is the last time we got together with our families on Thursday night and talked about what we hoped God would do in our Sunday service? When is the last time we actually took time to prepare our hearts for an encounter with God at church? You see, this question from my friend made me wonder if we really expect God to do anything at all in church. This question made me realize that sometimes all of us expect the pastor to be prepared and the musical worship team to be prepared but we just sit and expect others to take care of our worship. Our encounter with God has become the responsibility of someone else.

So as your next weekend approaches may I ask you to spend time in prayer preparing for what God has in store for you this Sunday? Will you take some time with your family and ask them what they are hoping God will do for them at church this week?

Will you spend time praying for your pastor and the church service asking God to meet with the congregation in a miraculous way?

Don't let church become another item on your to do list and simply check it off when the service ends. Become engaged in worship and prepare yourself and your family for what God has in store for you. What a shame it would be to miss what God has for us because we simply viewed our worship experience as another check off item on our list of tasks for the week. Make each worship service a time of awe as you have the joy and privilege of worshipping our remarkable God with your brothers and sisters in Christ.

# Building Monuments

I have been thinking about the faithfulness of God. There have been things in my life that I have been diligently praying about. One by one, I have seen God continuously answer my prayers. Yet, sometimes I move right on to the next thing...asking God now to intervene in my next troubling situation. Sometimes I even begin to forget about the many times God has previously answered my prayers.

I do believe that God realizes that the human mind is just naturally forgetful. After all, He made us. I am reminded in the fourth chapter of Joshua of how God commanded Joshua to create a memorial of twelve stones to remember how God helped Joshua and the people of Israel through a particularly difficult time. In fact, God said this to Joshua:

> Then Joshua said to the Israelites, 'In the future your children will ask, What do these stones mean? Then you can tell them, This is where the Israelites crossed the Jordan on dry ground (Joshua 4:21).

In other words, God is saying to create a memorial so that everyone will remember what God did here.

So what about you? Have you created any memorials just to remember what God has done for you? The next time God does something powerful in your life, I encourage you to get a small object to commemorate the occasion. Put it on your desk or a bookshelf. Every time you see it you will remember the power of God in your life and be encouraged. When someone asks you about the items, you will also have the opportunity to tell them about the power of God and the miracles He has performed in your life.

I suspect you will quickly develop a collection of memorials representing the work that God has done in your life. These memorials will serve as an encouragement to you as you continue to seek God.

Just like Joshua and his descendants, as you look at your collection of memorials you will always be reminded of God's faithfulness and his deep love for you.

# More Bad News

I am always amazed at the folks who stop me and want to talk about the most recent negative news reports. What will happen to the fiscal cliff our country is facing? Will the stock market crash? What will happen to my retirement? Have I heard about the latest shooting?

With twenty-four hour access to the news media we will always hear some bad news. But…as followers of Christ, why do we worry so much?

For my generation, there has always been bad news that causes us to worry. Do you remember these events?

> The 1963 assassination of President Kennedy
> The 1968 assassination of Martin Luther King, Jr.
> The 1972 Munich Olympic games massacre
> The 1974 oil crisis that caused the rationing of gasoline
> The 1979 Iranian hostage crisis
> The 1999 Columbine shootings
> The 2005 landfall of Hurricane Katrina
> The 2007 economic recession
> The 2012 Newtown shootings

You see…there is always something to worry about if we are looking for it. However, do you really think any of this bad news catches God by surprise? Do you really think God sits in heaven trying to figure out what He will do with all these situations? Is God just wringing His hands with worry? The answer is simple. Of course not!

Matthew 10:29 tells us:

What is the price of two sparrows—one copper coin? But not a single sparrow can fall to the ground without your Father knowing it. And the very hairs on your head are all numbered. So don't be afraid...

What a powerful verse! God is still in control of this world and this universe and He will take care of you. So stop worrying about the problems of this world and instead focus on the wonderful life God has given to you. Focus on those things that, with God's help, you can change to impact this world for the kingdom of God.

God is still in control!

# Napkin Notes

I read a story about a dad whose name is Garth. Garth was diagnosed with cancer for the third time. He was told by his medical team that he has an eight percent chance of living five more years. Garth is soon going to die. Imagine getting that type of news. Imagine looking across the desk at the doctor who tells you that your life is coming to an end. What would you do?

Garth decided he was going to do something special. He wrote 826 napkin notes with inspiring words for his daughter, Emma. He will have one note for his daughter's lunch for every day she is in high school. Let me give you an idea of what his notes say.

One note says this:

> Dear Emma, sometimes when I need a miracle I look into your eyes and realize I already created one. Love, Dad (Orme, "Dad").

So often we wait for tragedy to hit before we let people know how much we care about and love them. It's easy to get caught up in our own life pressures and forget what the Bible has told us. Take a look at James 4:14 that says:

> How do you know what your life will be like tomorrow? Your life is like the morning fog—it's here a little while, then it's gone.

The older I get the more I understand the truth in this verse. Life passes so quickly and there is no promise of tomorrow.

Let's not wait until it is too late to tell others how special they really are. Spend plenty of time with your family. Our children grow all too quickly. Our spouses are growing older each day. At some point, if we live healthy lives, our daily work jobs will be finished and I suspect most of us will wish we had spent more time on some of the things in our life with eternal significance. Go home tonight, hug your family and tell them how special they really are. Your family needs to hear it from you.

# How Well Do You Obey?

I always enjoy reading about the birth of Jesus. There are so many powerful lessons found in the birth of Christ but one that comes to mind is the power of obedience.

In the book of Luke, we learn that an angel appeared to Mary announcing that she would give birth to Jesus. Stop for a moment and don't miss the significance of this event. For you ladies, suppose you were to awaken in the middle of the night tonight. Next to you is an angel announcing you will give birth to the Son of God. What would you do? What would you be thinking? Mary spent some time in discussion with the angel and then simply said, *I am the Lord's servant. May everything you have said about me come true* (Luke 1:38).

What a response! Mary didn't engage in an argument with the angel. She didn't say how inconvenient this was going to be. She didn't say she was busy with other things. She didn't even say the timing just isn't good right now. Mary simply obeyed.

Mary wasn't alone in her desire to obey God. Joseph also had a significant part in this event. Now it's time for the guys to think about what you would do in this situation. Your girlfriend announces to you that she is pregnant and the baby's father is actually God. Do you believe it? What will you tell your family and friends? Maybe you should simply dissolve this relationship. This just doesn't seem to be working out for you.

Yet Joseph clearly supported and cared deeply for Mary. In fact, after the birth of Jesus, the book of Matthew tells us this:

An angel of the Lord appeared to Joseph in a dream. "Get up! Flee to Egypt with the child and his mother," the angel said. "Stay there until I tell you to return, because Herod is going to search for the child to kill him." That night Joseph left for Egypt with the child and Mary (Matthew 2:13).

I want you to focus on the critical words *that night*. Yes...*that night* Joseph left for Egypt. Joseph didn't question God about this directive. There was no hesitation. Joseph instantly obeyed.

So what is God telling you to do? Are you obeying? Often when God directs us to do something it may not be a convenient time, it may not be an easy situation, and it may not be something we even want to do. Still, when God speaks don't push Him aside. God is directing you for a reason. Don't forget the power in obedience.

# One Nation Under God

I frequently speak about school districts that surrender their beliefs after the simple threat of a lawsuit by groups such as the Freedom From Religion Foundation and the American Humanist Association. The administrative folks who represent these school districts need to develop some courage and take a stand for their religious liberty rather than so quickly give it away.

In spite of some of these school administrators, we are beginning to see some wonderful young people who have courage and are willing to take a stand for their beliefs.

Recently the American Humanist Association (AHA) filed a lawsuit in New Jersey. The AHA filed this lawsuit on behalf of a *family that objected to their child attending a school where the Pledge [of Allegiance] was said with under God included* (Gryboski).

Enter Samantha Jones. Samantha is a senior at Highland High School. Samantha sued to assure that she may continue to use the phrase *under God* when she says the Pledge of Allegiance. Samantha said this about her lawsuit:

> When I stand up, put my hand over my heart and say the Pledge of Allegiance, I am recognizing that my rights come from God, not from the government (Gryboski).

Samantha is up against a group that just can't take no for an answer. The American Humanist Association reminds me of the small child who just continues asking for something after their parents continue telling them no. You see, the Massachusetts' Supreme Judicial Court already ruled against the AHA in a similar lawsuit in the case of Doe v. Acton-Boxborough Regional School District. In this ruling the court said this:

> ...the recitation of the pledge, which is entirely voluntary, violated neither the Constitution nor the statute [which prohibits discrimination in Massachusetts public school education]... (Boycott)

But yet the AHA keeps pushing. They even launched a campaign called, *Don't Say the Pledge.* They are asking students to refuse to say the Pledge of Allegiance as long as it contains the words, *under God.* The AHA attorney said this:

> Until the pledge is restored to its inclusive version, we can take it upon ourselves to refuse to participate in what's become a discriminatory exercise (Boycott).

Wow! The Pledge of Allegiance is a discriminatory exercise? Did you ever think you would hear that?

I think our student, Samantha Jones, sums it up very well with this statement:

> If anyone wants to remain silent, that is their right. But it is not their right to silence me (Gryboski).

Well said, Samantha. AHA folks...just choose to remain silent if you don't want to say the Pledge of Allegiance. Stop acting like the child who has already been told no. I don't think many folks would mind not hearing from you.

# One Person Can Make a Difference

Do you ever wonder if just one person can really make a difference? Let's talk about one young lady who made a huge difference. Her name is Asia Canada. Asia is a cheerleader for Oneida High School in Oneida, Tennessee.

Since about 1930, Oneida High School has been saying a prayer before the start of their football games. Recently the Freedom From Religion Foundation (FFRF) and other atheist groups encouraged the school district to drop their prayer before the games. Again, like many school districts across the country, this school district immediately dropped the prayer at only the threat of legal action. The high school replaced the prayer with a moment of silence before the football games. Frankly, I have never understood what a moment of silence means but that's a topic for another time.

Well...enter the heroine of the story, Asia Canada. As the moment of silence is announced and quiet falls over the stadium, one voice rings out. That voice is coming from Asia Canada. Asia starts loudly reciting the Lord's Prayer...and it catches on. Soon the other cheerleaders have joined in, then the fans in the stadium. Even the opposing team members began reciting the Lord's Prayer. Can you imagine? What started as atheists demanding the elimination of prayer turns into a stadium of folks praying out loud.

Now before each home game Asia and the other cheerleaders say the Lord's Prayer. The FFRF really have nothing they can say about this since this prayer is not led by faculty or staff…it is student led.

The announcer for each of the Oneida High School football home games said this:

> Where you had one person saying a prayer over the PA, now you've got hundreds, maybe a thousand people saying it together (Hallowell).

So, maybe the Oneida School District and some of the other school districts that have caved in to the Freedom From Religion Foundation can become students again. Asia Canada just gave you a lesson if you're willing to listen. Don't be so quick to give in to those trying to take away our religious freedom. The solution isn't surrender. The solution is found in some creative thinking and having the courage to step up and take some action.

# Was America Founded
# on Christian Principles?

There are folks who constantly talk about the separation of church and State, and oppose prayer in our country. There are those who maintain that the United States was not founded on Christian principles and was never intended to be a Christian nation. Historian John Fea said:

> The idea that the United States is a Christian nation has always been central to American identity.

Fea said if the United States was not founded on the Christian religion *than someone forgot to tell the American people* (Fea).

As you think about prayer and the history of our country, remember that many of our most popular United States presidents supported prayer and a Biblical worldview.

Abraham Lincoln said:

> It is the duty of nations as well as of men to own their dependence upon the overruling power of God, and to confess their sins and transgressions in humble sorrow (Woolley, "Proclamation").

Ulysses S. Grant, said:

> Hold fast to the Bible as the sheet-anchor of your liberties; write its precepts in your hearts and practice them in your lives (Farstad).

Theodore Roosevelt had this to say about Biblical worldview and prayer:

Truth and righteousness are of no value to the world until they are embodied in a personality. And there is only one Source of Truth and Righteousness. Except as they flow from the Almighty God Himself, they do not exist (Dano).

Franklin D. Roosevelt asked the nation to join him in prayer on D-Day (OurDocuments).

Dwight D. Eisenhower stopped for prayer during his 1953 presidential inauguration (Dwight D. Eisenhower).

Ronald Reagan said this about prayer:

We must also seek help from God…our Father and preserver… the morality and values such faith implies are deeply imbedded in our national character ("Reagan").

If you hear folks say prayer is not a part of our country or even that our country has not been founded on Biblical principles, remind them to check their history. Even remind them what historian John Fea said…that if the United States was not founded on the Christian religion *than someone forgot to tell the American people.*

If our country was not founded on Christian principles and prayer is not an important element of those principles, I think they also forgot to tell our presidents.

# You Think You Have Problems

We all have problems and throughout our lives we will experience more problems of varying degrees. It just makes me shake my head when I observe followers of Christ who either don't believe they should experience problems or they complain loudly about the problems they are facing.

I remember the true story of a man who faced terrible adversity in his life. He lost his possessions. His farm workers were killed by criminals. His children were killed in a horrible accident. He lost his health. His friends asked him what sins he had committed in his life to cause all this anguish. He even lost the support of his wife who suggested that her husband just curse God and die. Do you know who I'm talking about? Yes...it's Job.

Even when confronted with all these problems here was Job's reply as recorded in the Bible:

> Should we accept only good things from the hand of God and never anything bad? So in all this, Job said nothing wrong (Job 2:10).

Isn't that a remarkable response? When is the last time we faced difficult issues and said to our family and friends, *Should we accept only good things from the hand of God and never anything bad?* What Job was really saying is this; If we are followers of Christ let's act like it. Let's be an example of the character of Christ.

Let's not complain like many in the world do. Let's not feel sorry for ourselves. Let's not quit and throw in the towel. Instead, let's understand that problems will be a part of life but we serve a God greater than our problems. Let's show others the joy that comes from following Christ. Let our behavior in the tough times cause others to ask why we are different. Let our examples be the motivation for others to develop a desire to also follow Christ.

# Pull Me Along

Horse shows are always entertaining. One show I attended involved young children and their horses competing in a variety of events. What really grabbed my attention were not the riding events but rather another type of competition. There were several events called *halter class* events where horses performed stunts while being directed by their handlers from the ground. I watched ten and eleven year old children make their horses trot, go in circles, and even walk backwards...using only a lead rope. In other words, these children were controlling eleven hundred pound horses with a small rope while walking next to the horses.

As I watched, I wondered why such a big creature like a horse would allow such small children to lead them when the horse could easily just refuse to obey orders and simply stand still. Those horses were so big and the children so small that the horses really could have done anything they wanted to do. Yet, the horses allowed themselves to be led and controlled by children with ropes. I can only believe that the horses just don't realize the power they possess. They don't understand that they possess tremendous muscle that would allow them to do just about anything they wanted to do. Instead, they follow instructions and are shackled only by a tiny piece of rope.

After watching these events, I found myself thinking about believers in Christ and thinking about some parallels to the horse competitions I just observed. I frequently see people, who claim to be followers of Christ, being led through life by events, people, or circumstances that leave them simply following and responding to things of this world. Like the horse on the rope being led by a child, these folks don't realize the power they possess through Christ Jesus. Rather than exercising the power of Christ, these folks are being led and directed by things of this world even when they possess the very spirit of God that allows them to break free of worldly pressures. As believers we don't need to be led around following the mandates of today's culture. We need to realize the power we possess through Jesus Christ and break free of our ropes to become the leaders Christ would ask us to be.

So when you are feeling out of control, helpless, unable to move on your own, and tugged by the ropes of the world, remember what the Bible tells us. Romans 8:11 says,

> The Spirit of God, who raised Jesus from the dead, lives in you.

Likewise, 1 Corinthians 3:16 tells us,

> Don't you realize that all of you together are the temple of God and that the Spirit of God lives in you?

This is a very powerful concept for all of us as believers. We are not designed to be led through life at the end of a rope. We are meant to show the world the power of Jesus Christ in our lives. The world is watching to see how believers in Christ live their lives. Let's not be the horse with the undiscovered power led by a rope throughout their life. Instead, let's follow what we see in 2 Timothy 1:7 that says, *For God has not given us a spirit of fear and timidity, but of power, love, and self-discipline.*

Let's be strong in Jesus Christ and a witness to the world of the power of God!

# The Reasons We Fail

Forbes Magazine published an article titled *10 Reasons Why We Fail*. Although many of these 10 reasons were quite interesting, one of the ten really intrigued me. Here it is:

People fail in their lives because others have convinced them of their station in life. Let me say it again, We fail because others have convinced us that we can't be more than we have already become (DiSalvo).

We would fail if we tried something harder. We would fail if we tried to become better fathers, mothers, children, employees, leaders, friends, or teachers.

This *station in life* concept is often thrust upon us by other people. They convince us that we are what we are and we just better live with it because we can never change.

John Maxwell, a prolific author on leadership, has a much more realistic approach to failure in his book *Failing Forward*. Maxwell says there is one major difference between average people and those who achieve great things. The difference is how the achievers respond to failure.

So if you have been convinced that you are to stay in your station of life, that to move forward would result in failure, I challenge you to listen to the words of Maxwell and *say good-bye to yesterday*. When you can change yourself you change your world.

As Christ tells us in the book of Proverbs 25:4:

Remove the impurities from silver and the sterling will be ready for the silversmith.

Let Christ remove your impurities through failure and learn from the experience. Strive to become sterling silver. Don't let failure from the outside impact you on the inside.

# Relax…I'll Drive

Do you remember the last time you were enjoying a peaceful drive and you suddenly realized someone was tailgating you? What was your reaction? Did you increase your speed? Did you slow down? Maybe you pulled over and let them pass you. Did you get angry or become nervous? Did you keep looking in your rearview mirror to keep an eye on them? Whatever you did, I suspect that you began to let the tailgater drive for you. You have probably been driving for years, you clearly know how to drive, and yet you found yourself in a position where you allowed someone else to dictate how you drive.

Let's talk about our lives. We clearly know how God has commanded us to live. Yet, at times, I bet you find your life being driven by something or someone else. Rather than following biblical principles, you find yourself accelerating and not waiting for God's direction, slowing down and missing opportunities, pulling over and giving up, or looking in your rearview mirror and letting your past haunt you. You are letting someone else drive your life.

I can't help but think of the story of Noah. God told him to build a boat for an impending flood. However, it had never rained before. Floods just didn't happen in Noah's time. Yet, Noah spent years building the boat that God had commanded him to build. I'm sure that neighbors laughed at Noah and made his life tough. They wanted to exert pressure to make him stop following God. You see, they wanted to drive for Noah. However, Noah was a man that followed God with his entire heart, and would never let others drive for him.

So, next time you experience a tailgater, rather than focusing on them, take some time to make sure you are following God's direction in your life and not allowing others to drive your spiritual car.

# Searching for God's Kingdom

I was reading a verse in Matthew that really made me think. In fact, you can find it in chapter 6, verse 33. Here is what the verse says:

> Seek the Kingdom of God above all else, and live righteously, and he will give you everything you need.

Let's focus on the first part of this verse...*seek the kingdom of God above all else.*

What you are seeking first in your life? Look at the marketing industry. They are trying to get your attention for all sorts of things. Cars, clothes, jewelry, food processors, cameras, computers...the list is endless. The marketing firms hope that they can convince you to put these things first in your life. In fact, a study by CBS News noted that each of us is exposed to about 5,000 ads every day. The world is fighting to get your attention and to take that attention away from seeking the kingdom of God first (Johnson).

May I encourage you to be deliberate about seeking the kingdom of God first in your lives? This doesn't happen by accident...there are too many things fighting for your attention. You must be deliberate in your quest to seek God.

What about the second part of this verse...*live righteously?* What does that even mean? Well, some other words for righteousness include decent, honest, right-minded, upright, and virtuous (Merriam Webster). How are you living your life? When folks think about you do those words come to mind? When your spouse and children think of you do those words come to mind? You see, this verse is a two-part verse. It's not a choice of either seeking the kingdom of God *or* righteousness. God has commanded each of us to seek the Kingdom of God *and* His righteousness.

This seeking of righteousness is never ending. Daily we must strive to follow the heart of God. We need to be careful about what we place into our heads. There is an old saying in the computer industry, *garbage in, garbage out*. It's the same with our desire for righteousness. We can't get there if we continue to place garbage into our minds. What does God tell us about our thoughts? One great example is found in Philippians 4:8:

> And now, dear brothers and sisters, one final thing. Fix your thoughts on what is true, and honorable, and right, and pure, and lovely, and admirable. Think about things that are excellent and worthy of praise.

So, if you're serious about seeking righteousness, here's a place to start...here is God's direction on how to think. Don't become obsessed with Ebola, ISIS, military actions, plane crashes, and the sad, shocking stories we hear about everyday.

Deliberately seek the Kingdom of God and His righteousness...think how God commands us to think...and your world will change remarkably. You will begin to live how God intended you to live.

# Collecting Shopping Carts

I had finished some shopping and was walking through the parking lot to my car. I spotted a man in the parking lot moving quickly to gather shopping carts that weren't properly placed in storage locations. It was a very cold night and this man was moving pretty quickly.

I had a chance to talk with him and told him he should be commended for gathering all these loose carts on a cold night like this. In our discussion, this man said that he had been looking out the window of the store and saw the store manager in the parking lot gathering carts. This man said that if the store manager is out here doing this work he should be too. Now here is a lesson for all of us, a lesson not just in leadership, but rather in our modeling of Christianity.

I frequently run into folks who tell me that they meet people who say they are followers of Christ but their life style says something different. People don't want to follow poor examples of Christianity. You know what? I have to agree. I see these same people. People who profess to follow Christ but have no joy in their life. They complain about everything. They lie, tell off-color jokes, manipulate to get their own way, and the list could go on. In fact, with some of these professing Christians it's hard to tell them apart from folks who claim no allegiance to the God of the Bible.

So let me take you back to the parking lot, the shopping carts, and the power of your example. When people see you do they notice something Christ-like about you? Like the shopping cart attendant watching his manager, do others see your Christian example and say, *I want what they have.* You see, when you claim to be a follower of Christ everyone is watching. Your co-workers are watching, your friends are watching, and your family is watching. You are the example and as a popular Christian song says, *you may be the only Jesus some people ever see.*

Am I saying you need to be perfect? Of course not. Nobody is perfect. Am I saying people should see Godly character in our lives? I sure am. Remember Matthew 7:16? Here is what it says:

> You can identify them by their fruit, that is, by the way they act.

Together let's make sure that people recognize us as followers of Christ by the way we act. Let's not have others watch us and just shake their heads in disappointment. Instead let's be examples of Godly character to everyone who sees us so that others say they want the power of God in their lives too.

# Dancing On the Edge of the Cliff

I am amazed at the number of folks who profess Christianity but choose to flirt with sin. They don't actually cross the line but they dance on the edge. In other words, they see how close they can get to sin without getting burned. This is a very dangerous behavior because the Bible tells us this will eventually draw us right into the middle of sin. Always remember Psalm 1:1 (King James Version) that says this:

> Blessed is the man who walks not in the counsel of the ungodly, nor stands in the path of sinners, nor sits in the seat of the scornful; but his delight is in the law of the Lord.

There is a very subtle progression in these verses that warn us about playing on the edges of sin. First, these verses caution us not to *walk* in the counsel of the ungodly. In other words, don't be *enticed* by sin in the first place. Stay clear and walk away. If you don't walk away while you can, the next portion of this passage says we will find ourselves *standing* in the path of sinners. You see, we were enticed by sin as we walked in the counsel of the ungodly and now we find ourselves stopped, standing and *engaged* in sin. Finally, this passage tells us if we didn't choose to get away, we will find ourselves *sitting* in the seat of the scornful. We have now *embraced* sin.

By flirting with sin, by playing along the edges of sin, we are beginning our walk down a path that will eventually lead us to sitting right in the middle of sin. We will follow the path described in Psalms. We will *walk* into sin. We will find ourselves *standing* in sin and eventually just *sit* down right in the middle of it. We have been enticed by sin, we have become engaged in the sin, and finally we find ourselves embracing the sin.

So what is the answer here? It's simple. Don't play around the edges of sin. Get away while you can and simply don't be enticed in the first place. Next time you are tempted by sin, remember to stop, turn around and run the other way. Do not be enticed. Do not become engaged in the sin. Don't embrace sin.

God has great plans for your life. Don't allow yourself to sit and get comfortable in the middle of sin and miss what God has planned for you.

# It's A Slow Fade

I remember a song I used to sing as a kid. I bet many of you sang it too. Here is one line from the song...

Be careful little eyes what you see.

As an adult I now realize the truth of those simple words. I see marriages crumble and families fall apart. I see folks actually believe the grass is greener on the other side of the fence. It's not.

A group called Casting Crowns wrote a song called *Slow Fade*. Here are some of the lines from their song:

Be careful little eyes what you see
It's the second glance that ties your hands as darkness pulls the strings

Be careful little feet where you go
For it's the little feet behind you that are sure to follow

It's a slow fade when you give yourself away
People never crumble in a day
Daddies never crumble in a day
Families never crumble in a day
It's a slow fade...(LaMendola)

So today let me say to you that a crushed life is often a slow fade. A divorce is a slow fade, a life filled with alcohol or drug dependency is a slow fade, adultery is a slow fade, moving away from following Christ is a slow fade. As Casting Crowns say, *People never crumble in a day*.

But a slow fade means there are many opportunities to stop the slide. You see there are probably hundreds of opportunities to stop a marriage from turning into a divorce. There are hundreds of opportunities to stop alcohol or drug abuse before it even starts. There are hundreds of opportunities to stop an inappropriate relationship before it starts. Where do all these opportunities start? How about with this one line...

Be careful little eyes what you see.

Next time you are tempted, sing that one line to yourself and remember...it's a slow fade.

# It's Time to Speak Up

It is time for followers of Christ to speak up. We have remained silent long enough and are paying the consequences of that silence. Groups such as the American Humanist Association (AHA) are forcing their way into areas that are far beyond where they should be going. In some instances the AHA has no right to push their beliefs but under the threat of a lawsuit many organizations give in without a fight.

In Gainesville, Georgia, the AHA took aim at Chestatee High School. The AHA sent a letter threatening a lawsuit against Hall County Schools because some of their coaches were praying with team members. The AHA claimed an unnamed *concerned citizen* had contacted them. So, one unnamed person is going to push around the entire Hall County School System? I don't think so...not in Hall County, Georgia. Here's a quote from a recent report about this incident.

> More than 200 people turned out in defiance of the self-described atheist group early Wednesday morning for an impromptu prayer rally in the middle of the Chestatee High School football field (Establishment).

Good for Chestatee High School! You see, organizations such as the AHA believe that a coach and student praying together is a clear violation of the Establishment Clause that sprung from the first amendment. But let's review the first amendment. Here is a portion:

Congress shall make no law respecting an establishment of religion, or prohibiting the free exercise thereof…(Establishment).

The AHA (and many groups like them) far over reach claiming the Establishment Clause covers far more than it actually does. They count on simple lawsuit threats to get their way. They are bullies. It is actually the AHA that is prohibiting the free exercise of religion in this case, not the staff and students at Chestatee High School.

In fact Chief Justice Rehnquist said this about intrusion into areas of religious liberty in a 2005 ruling:

[We] find no constitutional requirement which makes it necessary for government to be hostile to religion and to throw its weight against efforts to widen the effective scope of religious influence." Id. at 684 (citing Zorach v. Clauson, 343 U.S. 306, 313–14 (1952) (Van Orden).

The Chief Justice is right. The AHA wants the Hall County School System to be hostile towards religious freedom. We must do as the folks in Hall County are doing. Tell the atheist organizations that try to prohibit your exercise of religious freedom that you will not comply.

Representative Doug Collins of the ninth district in Georgia summed up this issue in Hall County with this statement:

This morning, while Chestatee students gathered on their football field to support their school leadership and exercise their rights, unspeakable human rights atrocities continued to happen across the world in places that have no regard at all for religious freedom. It's utterly disgusting that while innocent lives are being lost in Iraq and other places at the hands of radical religious terrorists, a bunch of Washington lawyers are finding the time to pick on kids in Northeast Georgia. I want the football players and all the students at CHS to know I support you, I'm here for you, and yes, I'm praying for you (Brown).

Just like the CHS faculty, staff, and students we must stand our ground and not let anyone rob us of our First Amendment right to exercise our religious freedom.

# Congested Area

I was driving through the mountains when a sign caught my attention. The sign read, *Congested Area Next 5 Miles*. Now I need to tell you…I was on a small two-lane road and had not seen a car coming in the opposite direction for miles. I am intrigued. What is going to cause this traffic congestion for the next five miles?

Well, five miles quickly passed and I noticed several apple orchards with corresponding stores but in the five miles I only counted six other cars on the road. Not exactly what I would define as a congested area.

That sign reminded me that much of what we think about is a matter of our unique perspective that may not actually be reality. Just as someone thought the road I described earlier was congested, each of us has perspectives about events in our lives.

Do you feel like your life is falling apart? Do you feel as though nobody really cares about you? Do you think your financial position can never be fixed? Perhaps your perspective on your situation just isn't reality. Jesus knew that at times we would all feel overwhelmed…that our perspective might not be in sync with reality. This is why Jesus said in Matthew 11:28:

> Come to me, all of you who are weary and carry heavy burdens, and I will give you rest.

Let Jesus put your life in the proper perspective. Then you can say good-bye to that *Congested Area* sign you are facing right now.

# The Star Spangled Banner Really Says This?

I often have people tell me that those involved in the early history of our country were not followers of the Christian faith. If I had more time I would go through a list of early leaders and presidents of our country and show you how fervently many of them believed in the God of the Bible. But with little time, I want to focus on just one of the folks who had such an impact on our country...Francis Scott Key. Francis Scott Key was an attorney and a poet who wrote the lyrics to what would become *The Star Spangled Banner*.

During the War of 1812, Francis Scott Key was asked to help negotiate the release of his friend, Dr. William Beanes, who had been captured by the British. That negotiation process had led Francis Scott Key to Baltimore and put him in a position to watch the British bombard Fort McHenry. After continual bombing, the British were not able to destroy the fort. However, at the conclusion of the attack on the fort, Francis Scott Key observed a large American flag being flown over the fort. He quickly penned the words for a poem called *The Defense of Ft. McHenry* that was widely published. Years later John Stafford Smith put this poem to music and it became what we now know as *The Star Spangled Banner* (Biography.com).

Most of us are familiar with the first verse of our national anthem. Here it is:

> Oh say can you see? By the dawn's early light.
> What so proudly we hailed at the twilight's last gleaming?

You know the rest of the verse.

We always hear the first verse but seldom hear the other three verses. I bet you didn't even know *The Star Spangled Banner* has four verses. Here is a portion of verse four:

> Blest with victory and peace, may the heav'n rescued land
> Praise the Power that hath made and preserved us a nation.
> Then conquer we must, when our cause it is just,
> And this be our motto: "In God is our trust."

History has recorded the faith in God that many of our country's founders and leaders have possessed. History has also recorded their prayers to God for our country.

Don't be fooled when people tell you our country has no history or foundation in God. I am thankful for people like Francis Scott Key who understood that we must put our trust in God...not in man.

Do your own research and you will be amazed at the wonderful Godly tradition of the United States of America.

# Surprise!

I am constantly hearing people talk about change. Folks usually talk about change as though it is some gradual event that we need to just ease into. Frankly, most changes that I have observed have not been gradual. The change has come as a surprise. A frightening diagnosis from the doctor, a spouse who wants a divorce, a death in the family, a child caught in the trap of sin...there is nothing for any of us to just ease into here. No time to sit back and get ready for it. One word sums it up...*surprise!* So rather than talk about being ready for change, I sometimes wonder if it would be better if we just said what we already know. Some difficult surprises will come into your life.

Now, how will you react to your surprises? Will you get angry, depressed, anxious, perhaps even start to question God's faithfulness? How many of you will start singing praises to God? Maybe that one isn't at the top of your list but let me take you to Acts chapter 16. Paul and Silas had just cast out a demon from a young girl and suddenly found themselves standing before city officials surrounded by a large crowd. Both men were beaten with wooden rods and then thrown into jail. Surprise!

The jails in this point in time were horrible places. A man by the name of Apablaza conducted a study called *Conditions of Prisons in the First Century*. Here are some of the things he found about prisons like the one Paul and Silas were in.

> Prisons were often packed beyond capacity resulting in unbearable heat and dehydration of prisoners.

> For security reasons the prisons had no windows often resulting in lack of air sometimes at a dangerous level.

Most prisons had no light and the psychological impact on prisoners was tremendous.

Prisoners were chained by their arms, legs or both. Each chain weighed about fourteen pounds and the weight would become debilitating.

Many of the dead would be piled in a corner of the jail to be taken away at a later time.

Yet, Paul and Silas are sitting in the dark, suffering the pain of a beating, chained, and they were singing hymns to God. As they are singing God performs a miracle that ultimately releases them from prison.

What are the lessons here? Surprises are coming. Don't ever lose hope in God. He does have a plan for you. Whatever you are facing today, trust in God and like Paul and Silas your miracle might be right around the corner.

# The Impact of Symbols

We all have favorite memories of special times that we often play back in our minds. We remember people who made a difference in our lives, our high school and college days, favorite teachers, great vacations, our wedding day, heart-warming moments with our kids, and the list goes on. We often collect items to remind us of these memories...a special Christmas ornament, an old letter from someone we loved, a favorite card, a shell from a beach vacation. We have a house full of items that are linked to wonderful memories.

What symbols are most meaningful to you? A wedding band? A favorite picture? An old Bible? One of your grown children's old stuffed animals? An old ticket stub from a special date? These items are so special that you only need to look at them and you are transported back in time to re-live that special time again. Symbols are important and we need to recognize their significance.

What symbols do you have to mark the times God remarkably touched your life? Look in the Bible at the book of Joshua. In chapter 4, God realized the importance of human memory and its relationship to the works of God. Joshua clearly understood the importance of symbols to remember God's touch in his life. He erected a stone memorial to honor one of God's miracles for the people of Israel so they would never forget what God did for them.

We all know that life has difficult times and that we need to have faith that God will provide. However, sometimes it is really tough to live by faith. To strengthen our faith, we sometimes need to take a look in our rear view mirror and remember what God did in our lives. Our memories reinforce the power of God and help us remember what God will do in our future.

Memories fade and we all need to keep symbols that remind us of God's faithfulness. Keep a journal, collect something special that reminds you of a difficult time and remember that God intervened and took care of you. Protect these simple memorials and when you are facing a difficult time pull them out and look at them. Read the journal where you can again remember the many times God has provided for you. Take out those special memorials you collected, hold them in your hands and remember the power of God.

Don't forget to look in your past to remember the power of God for your future.

# Take Down Your Sign

Dr. Tony Evans tells the story of a young man and wife who were injured in a car accident. The wife was severely injured and as the husband started looking around for help, he spotted a sign at the end of a nearby driveway that read, *William Smith, M.D.* The young husband carried his wife, who was now bleeding, to the front door of the doctor's house and knocked on the door. An older man answered the door and the husband said, *My wife is hurt very badly. You need to help her.* The doctor looked at the young couple and said, *I'm sorry. I don't practice medicine anymore.* The young man replied, *You either need to treat my wife or take down your sign.*

As Christians we are living in a world that is bleeding badly having been severely injured by sin. I can't remember a time in my lifetime that we have had so many secular worldviews, people trying to redefine the Biblical definition of marriage between one man and one woman, economics of our country turned upside down, and a world just suffering from the anxiety that comes from simply not knowing and following God.

It's time as followers of Christ that we start practicing the teachings of Christ or take down our sign. It's time for Christians to be Christians. It's time to speak into our culture and talk about issues in our culture that are clearly sin. We can't sit back and simply wait for someone else to do it. Time is short and if we don't speak up for Biblical truth, we will certainly miss our opportunity to have an impact.

So...what will you do? Be a Christian or take down your sign? I hope you decide to reinforce your sign and move full speed ahead for Jesus Christ and Biblical truth.

# Can You Help Me Find My Manners?

One evening my wife and I decided to go to a Japanese steak house. You know the type...where they cook the food right in front of you on a large hibachi grill. It's really dinner and a show as the chef does all sorts of wild things with the food to keep you entertained.

There were eight of us at the table. Six members of another family and my wife and I were sharing a large dinner table. We were all seated around the grill waiting for the show to start. The cook appeared and started the usual entertaining dinner antics but something even more interesting was occurring with the other family at the table.

The family having dinner with us had three teenage girls. One of the girls pulled out an iPad and set it up right in front of the grill. She wasn't concerned at all with the cook who was doing his best to entertain everyone. In fact, she wasn't even watching him. When her food was done the cook had to reach (with some difficulty) over the girl's iPad to get the food on her plate. The other two girls in the family pulled out phones and immediately began texting. Neither girl was watching the chef and both had no interest in what the chef was doing or saying. Mom, dad, and grandma said nothing as the girls typed away all through dinner.

Dinner was quite awkward as the chef did his best to cook a great meal and entertain a group of teens that clearly wanted no part of his entertainment. I noticed that at the conclusion of the meal the family hadn't spoken more than twenty words to each other.

This type of behavior is so common throughout our culture. I spoke with a young lady who displayed the skinned knees she received when she fell while she was walking and texting. I watched a video of a woman who walked off the side of a pier and fell into the ocean while she was texting. I watch people in church texting furiously while the pastor gives the Sunday morning message.

Parents, it's up to us to teach our children social skills and manners. The chef I spoke about earlier was clearly insulted by the activity of customers' texting throughout the meal. Many of us have also encountered rude behavior when people stop us in mid-sentence to answer a text.

If you want to make an impression today, put your phone away when you are at a social function. If someone invites you to dinner, focus on that person not your phone. If you are invited to someone's home, leave your phone in the car and engage in some conversation. Let people know you are interested in them, not your electronics.

It is our communication skills and our genuine concern for others that will impact the lives of others. If you really want to help someone, learn about them, and show them the love of Christ, put your phone away, look them in the eye and simply talk.

# Are You Really Thankful?

Life operates at a fast pace. We run from meeting to meeting, shuttle our children to events, and seldom have the chance to just slow down and relax. Our electronic devices have blurred the line between work time and recreational time. Frankly, we check our electronic devices far more than we should. Our calendars are full and free time is hard to find.

We need time to disconnect...time to pull the plug on some of our activities and simply reflect on our many blessings. As tough as we often view our busy lives, take time to remember that your hectic work life means you have a job. Your constant shuttling of children to their many events means you have a family to love and support. It is easy to get so busy that we just forget to slow down and be thankful for what we do have.

I am reminded of a story that illustrates our need to simply be thankful. Here it is:

> A blind boy sat on the steps of a building holding a sign that read: *I am blind, please help.* Next to the young boy was a box that contained a few coins that those passing by had placed inside.

> A man walked by the boy, took the sign, and wrote something on the other side. The man gave the sign back to the boy but now had the new words facing those who passed by.

> Soon the young boy's box began to fill up with money.

> Later the man who had changed the words on the sign returned to check on the boy. The blind boy recognized

his footsteps and asked, *Were you the one who changed my sign this morning? What did you write?*

The man told the young blind boy that he wrote the following words on the sign: *Today is a beautiful day but I cannot see it.*

You see, people who read the sign were thankful for their gift of sight and began giving to help the blind boy. They were giving out of thankfulness.

So instead of carrying your normal sign that says how busy you are, ask yourself what is beautiful in your life that you need to just stop and appreciate. Take some time to hug your family, give your co-workers a big smile, enjoy the gift of food during meals, turn off your cell phone, go for a walk with your spouse, read a book, take a nap, or just do whatever allows you to relax and be thankful for your many blessings.

Also remember 1 Thessalonians 5:18 that says:

Be thankful in all circumstances, for this is God's will for you who belong to Christ Jesus.

Be thankful!

# The Bible and Facebook

In 2006, CBS News conducted an interesting poll. They found that about 40 million people in the United States and Canada read the Bible every day. However, the poll also found that 143 million people in the United States and Canada are doing something else. What is it? They are actively using Facebook.

Let's fast forward to 2014. Facebook just celebrated their ten-year anniversary and reported that they now have 757 million daily active users. I realize that this figure includes folks from around the world but I wonder what the world would be like today if 757 million people read the Bible every day.

The Associated Press recently reported that about 400 billion photos have been shared on Facebook. If you printed out the pictures four to a page on regular-sized sheets of paper and put the paper end to end, it would stretch for about 17 million miles. That's enough paper to reach to the moon and back 34 times (Associate Press).

Based upon some of these survey numbers it is highly probable that many followers of Christ today reach for Facebook before they reach for their Bible (Casanova).

Now before you tell me that Facebook and social media are wonderful tools for reaching people for Christ, let me say I understand that. However, I really like what Jennifer LeClair wrote in an article for *Charisma News*. She said this:

> Somehow, even if Facebook were a part of mainstream Galilean culture, I don't think Jesus would give up

fellowship with the Father to check Facebook. It's become a near addiction for some people (LeClair).

Have you sacrificed fellowship with God to play Candy Crush or look at pictures on Facebook? Have you been neglecting Bible reading and now wonder why you don't hear God speaking to you anymore?

Maybe it's time for all of us to get our priorities straight. Next time you reach for Facebook ask yourself if you have had your time in the Bible yet that day. If you haven't, put Facebook away and pick up your Bible. It's probably time for you and God to exchange some status updates.

# Think About This

Some of my thoughts here are from a book titled, *Thinking For A Change* written by John Maxwell. In that book, Maxwell tells the story of two sisters. One sister just got word that she was accepted to the college of her choice. She was so excited to have earned the opportunity for a future career. The other sister leaned over to her mom and said this, *I feel so sorry for my sister. She has to go to school four more years!*

This story illustrates the underlying foundation of Maxwell's book. *Successful people think differently than unsuccessful people.* In our story, one sister thought about the wonderful opportunity she had been given to attend college and start a career. The other sister thought about all the time, effort, and work it would take to get through four years of college...two totally different ways of thinking.

What do you think about every day? Do you even take time to deliberately think about the future or are you just trying to get through the day. Maxwell says this about the power of thinking:

> Unsuccessful people focus their thinking on survival.
> Average people focus their thinking on maintenance.
> Successful people focus their thinking on progress.

If you aren't doing it yet, may I encourage you to spend some time each day deliberately thinking? A good way to get started is to spend some time at the end of each day reflecting on your day. Examine what was successful in your day. What decisions did you make that led to successful outcomes? What decisions did you make that led to negative outcomes? How could you have made your daily decisions better? If you will take fifteen minutes at the end of each day and reflect on the decisions you made during that day, you will learn tremendous lessons that you can use tomorrow.

Some of you may remember an old movie called *Groundhog Day*. In that movie, the main character continues to live the same day over and over again. I hope you aren't trapped in a similar situation. If you feel like you are simply repeating your workdays, break free by thinking deliberately each day, learn from the lessons of the day that God is teaching you, and apply new ideas to your life.

Former General Electric CEO, Jack Welch once said, *99.9% of all employees are in the pile because they don't think* (Maxwell, *Thinking*). Don't be one of many struggling in the employee pile. Spend some time thinking and live the exciting, creative life God has planned for you.

# It's Time to Take Out the Trash

Have you watched the news recently and just been depressed when it ended? I was recently looking at the headlines and remembered again why I don't spend much time there. I sure don't find many stories that make my life richer.

I really don't care how much jail time rapper Chris Brown received this week. Although I must confess, he is a great reminder that money isn't everything. Here is a guy worth an estimated quarter of a billion dollars and he can't get his life together.

I really don't care about what product Lady Gaga will use for her next dress. Is it raw beef or some other equally appalling product used to gain our attention? And, yes, she did make a dress from raw beef.

I don't want to know all the details on the latest mass murder that took place somewhere in the world. Knowing every detail won't make my life happier.

So what interests me? A remarkable teacher like Julie Bauchman who arranged a big surprise for one of her students interests me. Mrs. Bauchman's little kindergartener hadn't seen her military dad since he was deployed two years ago. Mrs. Bauchman made a wonderful surprise reunion happen ("You'll Cry When She Sees Soldier Dad").

What about the man in China who every day carries his disabled son eighteen miles a day to school and back because he just won't give up on his son (Dailymail).

Stories like these inspire me and make me say *way to go* to people like Mrs. Bauchman and the dad from China. These folks are making a big difference in the lives of others…even if it is only one person.

Should it surprise us that positive news gives us a lift and negative news makes us depressed? I don't think so. Let me take you to Philippians 4:8 that says:

> And now, dear brothers and sisters, one final thing. Fix your thoughts on what is true, and honorable, and right, and pure, and lovely, and admirable. Think about things that are excellent and worthy of praise.

God knew all along that filling our minds with trash would harm us and He gave us clear instructions on what to think about. Next time you sense trash going into your head, grab your TV remote control and turn it off. Take control of your computer and look at something else. Do what God has commanded and think about things that are excellent and worthy of praise. It will make a huge difference in your life.

# Do You Really Trust God?

How much do you trust Jesus?  Think about it...how much do you *really* trust Him? Do you remember the song, *'Tis So Sweet to Trust In Jesus*? It's a familiar song to many in the church.  If you don't know it, the chorus of the song goes like this:

> Jesus, Jesus, how I trust Him!
> How I've proved Him o're and o're
> Jesus, Jesus, precious Jesus
> Oh for grace to trust Him more.

In 1882, Louisa Stead, her husband, and daughter Lilly went for a picnic on Long Island Sound. As they were eating lunch they heard screams coming from a drowning boy.  Mr. Stead ran into the water to save the boy.  Instead of saving him, Louisa and Lilly watched their husband and father drown as the struggling boy pulled him under the water.

Louisa and Lilly were left destitute...no money and very little food. Their primary means of support was dead and they were on their own.  Eventually, people in the community began to leave food at their door and Louisa became overcome by God's provision for her and Lilly. After trusting God to provide for each day, after trusting God to heal the pain from losing her husband, after trusting God to put joy back in her life, Louisa sat at a table in her meager house. There she wrote the words to the song we just talked about, *'Tis So Sweet To Trust In Jesus* (Get Beyond).

Now let me ask you again: how much do you really trust Jesus with your entire life?  Proverbs 3:5 tells us:

Trust in the Lord with all your heart; do not depend on your own understanding.

In other words, God is in control of everything in your life. God didn't say trust in Him with *part* of your heart. He said trust in Him with *all* of your heart. Don't try to understand everything that happens in your life. You never will understand it but you can be assured that God is with you if you will simply trust Him.

Are you having financial issues? Trust God. Are you going through tough times in your marriage? Trust God. Are you suffering health issues? Trust God. Have you lost your job? Trust God. Whatever it is you are facing, let me say it again...trust God. When you trust Him, you will experience the same remarkable touch of God that Louisa Stead experienced and you will really mean it when you say, *'Tis so sweet to trust in Jesus.*

# What You Do Today
# Can Change Your Future

A few years ago, John Maxwell wrote a fascinating book called, *Today Matters*. In that book Maxwell noted that what we do with our time each day will determine our future. I believe Maxwell is right.

According to Reuters News, Americans watch an average of nearly thirty-five hours of TV each week. That's almost equal to a full-time job. In the average home, there are more television sets than people (Thomasch).

According to another survey by America Online and Salary.com, American workers are wasting almost two hours of every eight-hour workday, and that doesn't include lunch or scheduled break time (Malachowski).

This study also revealed the following about employees:

31% waste roughly 30 minutes daily
31% waste roughly 1 hour daily
16% waste roughly 2 hours daily
6% waste roughly 3 hours daily
2% waste roughly 4 hours daily
2% waste 5 or more hours daily

This means that 4% of the people surveyed waste at least half the average workday!

I suspect if you asked those watching thirty five hours of TV or those wasting time surfing the Internet to tell you about their life plans, they would tell you that they always wanted to start their own business but just don't have the time. Or perhaps they just don't understand why they can't seem to get promoted at work. I bet you would hear an endless stream of excuses for why these folks can't seem to get ahead.

The answer is very simple and Maxwell is right. Here's the answer again in case you missed it...*Today Matters*. How you spend your day each and every day will determine your future. You will never get today back again.

So what will it be? Watch TV or spend time with your family? Surf the Internet or think of ways to be productive and help your company advance? Check Facebook or read your Bible? You see, your day really is yours. You get to decide how your day will unfold. Choose wisely because today really does matter.

# Loaded With a Hair Trigger

With all that has been in the news recently about gun control, I began to think about a weapon we all possess that has done tremendous damage to others. This weapon has cut deeply into the spirits of others, has severed relationships, has left people devastated and in tears, has fired numerous shots, and can be re-loaded in an instant. What is the weapon? The weapon is your tongue.

The Book of James says many things about the tongue. In chapter 3, verse 5, we read this:

> But a tiny spark can set a great forest on fire. And the tongue is a flame of fire. It is a whole world of wickedness, corrupting your entire body. It can set your whole life on fire…

Have you ever had your tongue set your life on fire? Have you ever said something and the moment you said it just wished you could take it back? Maybe it was something you said to your spouse this morning. As soon as you said it, you could see the look of hurt in their eyes. Perhaps you said something cutting or hurtful to your child and saw a tear start to form. Maybe you made a careless remark to a co-worker years ago and now you are enemies seeking to cause trouble for each other.

Once you say something you can never get it back. You may ask for forgiveness but the damage is already done.

As you go through this week remember that you possess a weapon that can truly set your life on fire as well as the lives of others. As you continue to seek and develop the character of

Christ, don't let your tongue get in the way of your example to others. When someone upsets you stop, take a breath, and think about your response before you engage your weapon. Refuse to simply fire randomly. Allow the Holy Spirit to help you perfect a Godly aim.

You can use your tongue to build up others, diffuse tense situations, develop wonderful relationships, and demonstrate the love and power found in Christ. So use your tongue to snuff the fires going on in the lives of others and refuse to allow your tongue to be the match that starts fires in those around you.

# Experiencing Tunnel Vision

As I was driving to work I saw a man calmly sitting on his front porch. Now that might not seem unusual unless you saw how he was sitting. He was in a chair, drinking his morning coffee but he was seated facing his front door. Instead of enjoying the beautiful view from his porch, he was staring at his door.

Now, he may have had a good reason to be sitting like this but his unusual positioning painted a perfect picture for the way many of us view life. Rather than taking in the full view of life, we focus on one problem and develop tunnel vision. Tunnel vision is a term used to describe what we tend to see when we are under stress. Our vision is constricted…just as if we were looking through a long tunnel. We can see that small, narrow view but anything beyond that is simply ignored. Isn't that often the way we view life? We can't see anything except for that one problem right in front of us. In fact, the answer to our problem might become obvious if we simply widened our view.

I'm reminded of the story of the disciples caught in the terrible storm while crossing the Sea of Galilee. The disciples were so caught up in the problem of the storm that they forgot the answer to their problem was asleep in the back of the boat. When the disciples finally looked beyond their storm and widened their view, Jesus answered their request. In Mark 4:39, we read:

> When Jesus woke up, he rebuked the wind, and said to the waves, 'Silence! Be still!!' Suddenly the wind stopped, and there was a great calm.

As you face problems that surface in your life, remember not to develop tunnel vision and be like that man who stared at his front door. Widen your view and remember that just as Jesus calmed the storm on the Sea of Galilee, He can calm the storms in your life.

# The Search for Water

Have you ever watched someone water flowers? As I watched this process I began to think about the power of water. Not the water you and I might ordinarily think about on a hot summer day but rather the living water we read about in the Bible.

When I was younger we used to sing a song in church that said this:

> Like the woman at the well I was seeking for things that would not satisfy. But then I heard the Master saying draw from the well that never will run dry.

That song is talking about the Bible story we read in John chapter 4. In this account, Jesus is talking to a woman filling her container at a well. She has come there to draw water to drink but she is about to encounter the power of God. This woman has quite a story and must have been pretty disillusioned with her life. In fact, this scripture tells us that the woman had five husbands and the man she was living with was not her husband. She has been searching for earthly things to satisfy her spiritual needs.

As Jesus and the woman were talking about the water in the well, Jesus says this to the woman:

> Anyone who drinks this water will soon become thirsty again. But those who drink the water I give will never be thirsty again. It becomes a fresh, bubbling spring within them, giving them eternal life (John 4:14).

So, how about you?  Are you like the woman at the well looking for things of this world that just don't satisfy your soul? Are you caught in the trap of trying to gain money and possessions?  Do you find yourself searching for romantic relationships that continue to fail?  Are you caught in the trap of alcohol or drugs…like the woman at the well just looking for something to satisfy your soul?

If you find yourself caught in these traps, you need a drink of eternal water.  In other words, let Jesus change your life. Give Him a chance to change you from the inside out.  It really is easy. Simply ask Jesus to forgive you of your sins and become the leader of your life.  Then watch your life begin to change as God now directs your steps and satisfies your soul as only He can do.

# The Gift of Kindness

WestJet, a Canadian airline, did something spectacular one year for Christmas. As passengers checked in for a flight between two cities in Canada, Santa was at check in to ask each person what they wanted for Christmas. Each passenger had something special they wanted. One wanted a camera. A small child wanted a train. Another man wanted socks and underwear. One family wanted a big television set. After giving Santa their Christmas wish, the passengers boarded their flight thinking nothing more about their requests.

However, while the flight was in the air, WestJet staff members sent out teams to buy every item that had been requested when the passengers checked in for the flight. The teams bought all the gifts, wrapped them, and were waiting with the surprises as the flight landed.

Instead of luggage coming from the baggage carousel, the passengers were greeted with wrapped gifts with their names on them. Passengers received just what they had asked for at check in...including the family who wanted the large television set. That family received a fifty-inch flat screen TV (Orme, "I've Never Seen").

Holidays come and go but kindness toward others, like that shown by WestJet, doesn't need to stop. We may not be able to buy a plane full of gifts for others but we can choose to help people every day. All year long we see children in our community who need food. All year long we encounter parents who don't know how they will pay this month's bills. All year long we meet folks who just need someone to listen to what they are going through and maybe offer a little advice. All year long we run into people who just need a friend. They don't always need your money...they need your love.

We're reminded of this in I Corinthians 13:13 that says:

> Three things will last forever--faith, hope, and love--and the greatest of these is love.

Remember, some of the most important gifts you can give to others involve no money. They simply involve you choosing to invest in the lives of others. So, watch for opportunities to love others. When you see an opportunity, go ahead and take a risk. Investing and loving others really is a wise investment and will pay far greater dividends than any financial investment you will ever make.

# What Really Scares You?

If today I asked you what you fear, how would you answer? What are those things in your life that really scare you? I'm not talking about spiders or the dark, I'm talking about fears that you face as a part of who you are. Deep inside, what really scares you? Death, sickness, a ruined career, financial devastation...what is your secret fear?

During the American Civil War battles, General Stonewall Jackson always had the habit of riding his horse right on the lines where the shooting took place. Bullets hit all around him. His aides were frequently trying to get Jackson to move to the back and direct the fighting from there. Yet, General Jackson would never move to the back of the line. He was always right out in front encouraging the troops and giving directions. Finally, one of Jackson's aides again urged General Jackson to move to the rear and here is Jackson's response:

> Captain, my religious belief teaches me to feel as safe in battle as in bed. God has fixed the time for my death. I do not concern myself about that, but to be always ready, no matter when it may overtake me. Captain, that is the way all men should live, and then all would be equally brave (Selby).

Maybe General Jackson was on to something. Maybe we fear because we are trying to take control when we should be turning the control of our lives over to God. Perhaps deep down inside we all know that we can't control much of anything that has real eternal significance. We need God in our lives. We need to acknowledge that it is God who has ultimate control and not us.

I suspect that as we release control of our lives to God, we also hand over our fear. Those fears that nag at us will start to disappear. I am reminded of Philippians 4:6-7 that says this:

> Don't worry about anything; instead, pray about everything. Tell God what you need, and thank him for all he has done. Then you will experience God's peace, which exceeds anything we can understand.

Are you looking for relief from your fears and the chance to experience God's peace? Be like General Stonewall Jackson and turn your fear over to God. Then you can truly focus on the exciting life God has planned for you instead of spending each day of your life in fear and worry.

# Oh...Whatever

As I talk with and listen to people all over the country, I am amazed to hear one word used over and over in conversations. This word really is associated with life in a postmodern world. What is the word? Here it is...*whatever*.

When people are confronted with something they don't want to hear or disagree with the response is inevitably *whatever*. In other words, if it works for you and doesn't harm them leave it alone. There is no reason to confront anyone over his or her beliefs. Remember the old saying, *Live and let live?* That is just what we are talking about here. Rather than confront people for their inappropriate behaviors or actions we choose to ignore it, turn our heads, and walk away simply saying, *whatever*. If I could pick one word that best represents a postmodern worldview it would be that single word.

But the Bible clearly gives us guidance for everyday living. There are absolute truths...those things that God clearly tells us to do or not to do...those behaviors that are clearly sin. There are behaviors and actions that God tells us will harm or strengthen us. The scriptures make it very clear how Christians must behave. In the Christian worldview there is no room for *whatever*.

God has clearly told us in 1 Peter, 3:15:

> Instead, you must worship Christ as Lord of your life. And if someone asks about your Christian hope, always be ready to explain it. But do this in a gentle and respectful way.

So next time someone tells you *whatever*, don't let them sidestep the conversation so easily. Stop them and ask them what they mean. Gracefully engage them in conversation. See if you can probe deeper and give your conversation some meaning. Clearly let others know what Christ can do in their lives and seek every opportunity to *speak up and tell anyone who asks why you're living the way you are.*

# Who Do You Want To Be?

Have you ever asked yourself who you really want to be? Notice I didn't ask you *what* you want to be but rather *who* do you want to be?

When I am at social gatherings it is amusing for me to watch the interaction among people. After learning someone's name, men generally follow up with the second question. So, what do you do?

We live in a world where our worth is often linked to our job. However, we know that nothing could be further from the truth. We see people every day who have high power jobs but yet are falling prey to the sins of the world. A United States president accused of involvement in Watergate who ultimately resigned. Another U.S. president accused of an inappropriate relationship with an intern. A military general accused of an inappropriate relationship with a business associate. Business executives indicted for criminal activity. These folks know **what** they want to be but they have struggled with **who** they want to be.

When I think of someone who clearly knew *who* he wanted to be, I can't help but think of the life of Joseph, detailed in the book of Genesis. Here is a young man who was tempted with sexual immorality by the wife of his boss. Even when tempted Joseph replied to her,

> How could I do such a wicked thing? It would be a great sin against God (Genesis 39:9).

Joseph understood who he wanted to be. He wanted to be a man that followed after the heart of God. He wasn't about to let anything destroy his relationship with his God.

So who do you want to be? Do you want to follow after the desires of man or do you want to follow the character of Christ? Follow God or follow man? You must pick one. You can't serve both.

I hope you make the decision about who you want to be. Be that person who pursues a relationship with God and builds their character on solid Godly principles.

# Why This Accident Made Me Smile

I was on my way home from work and was stopped at a red light. The car at the light in front of me was also stopped and blocking much of the entrance to a business I was trying to enter. I was trying to figure out if there was enough room between my car and the one in front of me so that I could squeeze into the parking lot.

As I was making those mental measurements, I was suddenly thrown forward and caught by my seatbelt. A quick glance in my mirror and I realized a truck had just smashed into the back of my car and was pushing me into the car in front of me. I heard metal bending, saw steam start to come from under my hood and felt the pain from being thrown forward at a high velocity.

The end of the story is that a driver coming up behind me hadn't realized that everyone was stopped at the red light and had just slammed into my car pushing me into the car in front of me. In short order the police, fire, and ambulance were on the scene and the little area of the street was a flurry of activity. It was a hot day and I was standing on the sidewalk watching all the activity. A woman from one of the shops along the street came up to me and asked if she could get me a glass of cold water. All of a sudden my mind left the accident and focused on the kindness of this woman. She didn't have to leave what she was doing and come check on me. She made the offer out of kindness.

Remember the verse in Matthew 10:42 that says this:

> And if you give even a cup of cold water to one of the least of my followers, you will surely be rewarded.

You see, I'm certain Christ really knew the impact of giving to someone else...the power of simple kindness. When the woman at the accident asked me if I wanted some cold water, it really wasn't about the water. It was about a woman showing an act of kindness to someone she didn't even know. At that moment there were no racial differences, social status concerns, or philosophical differences. There was simply a woman who wanted to show she cared about me and extended an offer to help.

I'll never know this woman's name but she has made me look at Matthew chapter 10 through totally different eyes. I hope that as you have opportunities, you, too, will offer a cup of water whenever you can.

# Winning the Fight

Have you ever found yourself more interested in winning the argument than making the right decision? At one point in my life I worked with a man who simply had to win any and all discussions. All issues became battles of logic rather than seeking Godly wisdom to select the best course of action to resolve the issues. At the end of most encounters with him I felt the energy in me drain away. I wasn't energized and excited by my encounters with him. Instead I was tired and worn down.

We all know how disheartening and non-productive it is to engage folks who are simply impressed with their own wisdom. We live in a world full of folks who always demand something from you, very vocally give their opinions when nobody asked, continually tell you about themselves and the wonderful things they are doing, and the list could go on and on.

Laurie Beth Jones in her book titled *Jesus, CEO* called people like this *energy leaks*. You know the people I am talking about. When you see them in a store you quickly walk down another aisle. When you see them on the street you quickly cross to the other side. When you see them in the parking lot you take your spouse by the hand and lead them quickly to your car as you start to feel the energy being pulled right out of your body.

God has not called us to be energy leaks. In fact, Proverbs 3:7 tells us:

> Don't be impressed with your own wisdom. Instead fear the Lord and turn away from evil.

So...as followers of Christ let's exhibit Godly wisdom to others. When Christ talked about being *light and salt* he was speaking about building the lives of others...leaving others stronger, happier, joyful, and energized after seeing and encountering the power of God in us.

So which are you today...energy leak or Godly energy source? I hope you will seek to become an energy source that others want to be around and follow because they see something special in you. We know that special something they see in you is the amazing power of God working in a Christian life!

# May I Borrow a Cup of Worry?

Are you a worrier? Do you always look for the trouble that you just know is coming your way? As I talk with people, I encounter folks who just can't help but worry. They worry about their health, their job, their finances, the presentation they are giving the next day, what they should wear, whether people will like them. Some even worry whether their plane is going to crash as they head off for vacation. When many people start worrying they find it almost impossible to stop.

How much trouble do you borrow from tomorrow? Do you spend a lot of mental energy worrying about things that will never happen? I am reminded of an anonymous quote that said this:

> I am an old man and have known a great many troubles, but most of them never happened.

You know what? This quote is accurate. We worry about things that simply never happen.

In Philippians 4:6-7, the Bible says this about worry:

> Don't worry about anything; instead, pray about everything. Tell God what you need, and thank him for all he has done. Then you will experience God's peace, which exceeds anything we can understand.

So, stop worrying about things that will never happen. Stop borrowing trouble from tomorrow. Follow what the Bible teaches us about worry and you will sleep better, enjoy better relationships with family and friends, perform better at work, enjoy life more, and just have more fun.

I agree with Mary Crowley who said this about worry:

> Every evening I turn my worries over to God. He's going to be up all night anyway (Bachan 130).

# White Covers It All

After a beautiful snowfall I was standing with my wife in our dining room looking at the newly fallen snow. We were talking about how our normal view out of this window had changed. The view was new. The white snow had transformed the woods into something even prettier and certainly much different.

As I thought more about this, I remembered places that weren't so pretty to see without the covering of snow. Some were run down, broken, and falling apart. Yet, when covered by the snow these areas became new. These places became beautiful. Old buildings and run down neighborhoods were transformed by the covering of the white snow.

The color white has some interesting history. In ancient times people on trial for crimes were given a white stone if they were acquitted and found innocent. The color white symbolized that innocence (Got Questions).

If you study the psychology of colors you will find that white is the color of new beginnings and of wiping the slate clean. Some psychologists say that white symbolizes a blank canvas just waiting to be written upon.

It is no wonder that we read this in Isaiah 1:18 when Christ says:

> Though your sins are like scarlet, I will make them as white as snow. Though they are red like crimson, I will make them as white as wool.

You see, just like run down, dilapidated buildings there are those with run down and dilapidated lives. Lives that are broken.

Lives that aren't pretty to see. Lives filled with sin like scarlet that need to be made beautiful again and white as snow.

By letting Christ become the leader of your life, your sins are forgiven and that white color we have been talking about symbolizes a new beginning for you. Your old life filled with sin has been wiped clean and you are ready for a new beginning. Your life has now become a blank canvas just waiting for the artistry of God to make you a new person.

Are you ready for a new beginning? Today is the day. This is the moment. Though your sins are like scarlet, Christ will make them white as snow. Don't wait. Ask God to wipe your old slate clean today and experience a new beginning in Christ.

# That Will Leave a Mark

The area of the country where I live sometimes faces icy weather conditions. Radio and TV broadcasts caution all of us to drive safely on slippery roads. Friends tell me to be careful while walking to avoid a fall. We put chemicals on steps and roads to melt the ice and avoid accidents.

What struck me is that as careful as everyone tries to be during the icy conditions, we just seem to be so amused when someone finally does fall. When I served as a police officer I remember getting dispatched to an accident in very icy weather. When I arrived, people were standing around smashed cars all watching me get out of the police car. I carefully adjusted my Smokey the Bear hat, opened the car door, took about two steps and promptly slid down a ten-foot embankment smashing my hat as I rolled down the hill. It was so slippery that I had to get the help of the people involved in the accident to pull me back up the embankment. I can tell you this...the folks involved in the accident were absolutely hysterical watching me roll down the hill. In fact, it was so funny to them that they didn't even ask if I was OK. They simply enjoyed the show.

We have entire TV shows that are dedicated to showing videos of people falling off bikes, trampolines, horses, boat docks, and skateboards. These videos even provide monetary awards for the best fall according to an audience vote. We sit in our living rooms laughing over these falls that often look quite painful.

I just don't know what it is but we find it funny when people fall. We say things like, *I bet that hurt* or *that will leave a mark* and then have a good laugh.

But let me say this. We have people that we interact with every day that are in another type of fall...a spiritual fall. Sometimes I wonder if we observe folks struggling with their faith and experiencing a spiritual free fall and treat it almost like a physical fall. We see folks whose lives are spinning out of control because they have rejected Christ...they are falling...and we simply ignore them or think to ourselves, *that will leave a mark*. We see people spiritually falling and struggling all around us, recognize their need for Christ, but yet we do nothing.

I am reminded of Matthew 28:19-20 that says:

> Therefore, go and make disciples of all the nations, baptizing them in the name of the Father and the Son and the Holy Spirit. Teach these new disciples to obey all the commands I have given you.

So...when you see folks in a spiritual free fall get involved. Do what Christ commanded...go and make disciples. In other words, tell falling folks about the wonderful power of God and what their life could be like if they allowed Christ to be their leader. Step in and be their spiritual guardrail, helping hand, safety net, or whatever it takes to break their spiritual fall. We live in a world of spiritually falling folks who desperately need you to show them how the power of Christ can stop their fall. There are some folks that you can reach better than anyone else. Get involved and don't let people fall.

# Are You a Critic or Encourager?

I was on an airplane watching all the folks doing the things you do to prepare for takeoff. Some passengers were already seated and others were coming into the plane, putting their carry on items away, and others simply finding their seats.

During this boarding process a young lady was in the aisle trying to put her small carry on in one of the overhead compartments. The flight was crowded and this lady was trying to wedge her small piece of luggage into the overhead.

As she was completing this task, a man in the seat in front of me said in a very loud voice, *you wouldn't have all that trouble with your luggage if you didn't bring so much junk."* Suddenly the buzz of talking in my seating area stopped and everyone was looking at each other to see if they really heard what they thought they heard. Everyone waited for the woman's response but she just found her seat and didn't say a thing.

Let me contrast this man's behavior with another woman I encountered that same day. I noticed this woman in the train that left the gate area and went to the baggage claim. She was an airport employee who was wearing headphones and just dancing and smiling…simply enjoying life. When I smiled at her she took off her headphones and with a big grin said this to me:

Sometimes you just have to dance.

So which person are you? Are you like the man on the plane…a critic? Or are you like the dancing woman…an encourager? You see we live in a world of critics. We're surrounded by folks who believe they always know what is best for us and are willing to quickly critique our actions. We see critics on the news, at sporting events, in our churches, and often in our homes.

Let me simply say this, the world doesn't need more critics. We have plenty of them. We need encouragers. We need folks that really have the joy of the Lord and show it even when they are not intentionally trying to show it. The joy of the Lord is in them and just bubbles out. We need more people like the dancer who make us smile just by being around them. Frankly, we need fewer people like the critic in the plane.

If we really are followers of Christ let's show the world the joy we have found in Christ. I'm reminded of Galatians 5:22 that says:

> But the fruit of the Spirit is love, joy, peace, patience, kindness, goodness, faithfulness…

So today decide to be an encourager. Let's show others some spiritual fruit. Show the world the joy that is only found in Christ and let them be excited and uplifted by your encouragement…not disappointed by your critique.

# Arise My Love

Musical artists *NewSong* sing a remarkable song titled, *Arise My Love*. As you listen to the lyrics of that song there is a very powerful sentence that says this:

The grave no longer has a hold on you.

Think about that sentence for a moment…the grave no longer has a hold on you. This one sentence carries tremendous power and truth for the followers of Christ. We no longer have the shackles of sin or the sting of death hanging over us.

Often we carry our past around with us like shackles, chained to old memories and actions that haunt us and shake our self worth. May I tell you something? As a follower of Christ, the grave no longer has a hold on you. Your past sins have been forgiven, removed, and sent as far as the east is from the west. Live in confidence and enjoy a life filled with the power of Christ.

Perhaps you're not a follower of Christ and sin still does have a hold on you today. The Bible tells us that we have all sinned. If you have never confessed your sins to God and asked for forgiveness, the Bible also makes it very clear that the end result of sin is death.

Here's the good news. Christ has already paid the price for our sins on the cross. He died on the cross for all our sins. Christ did that so the grave would no longer have a hold on anyone. All we need to do is admit that Jesus is Lord and that God raised Him from the dead. The Bible tells us that everyone who calls on the name of the Lord will be saved.

C.S. Lewis says this about death:

> Has this world been so kind to you that you should leave with regret? There are better things ahead than any we leave behind (Lewis).

Lewis is right. There is no longer any sting of death if you are a follower of Christ. Death is simply the entry point for an eternity with God.

Don't wait any longer…ask Jesus to be the leader of your life and experience a new life filled with the joy and freedom that comes from living for Christ. Then you can truly say that the grave no longer has a hold on you.

# References

Aldrin, Buzz. "Guidepost Classics: Buzz Aldrin on Communion in Space." Guideposts. 2016: n.page. Web.

Apablaza, Simon. "Conditions of Prisons in the First Century." *Scribd*.Web

Associated Press. "Facebook Beats the Bible in Daily Readers." *Tampa Bay Times*. 4 February 2014; n.page. Web.

Bains, G.S.; LS Berk, N Daher, E Lohman, E Schwad, J Petrofsky, and P Deshpande. "The Effect of Humor on short-term memory in older adults: a new component for whole-person wellness." *US National Library of Medicine*. National Institutes of Health. Spring; 28(2): 16-24. 2014; n.page. Web

Barna Group Inc. "Most Americans Consider Easter a Religious Holiday, But Fewer Correctly Identify its Meaning." *BarnaGroup Inc.* 15 March 2010; n.page. Web.

Biography.com, Ed. "Francis Scott Key Biography." *A&E Television Network*. 19 September 2016. Web.

Brown, Tim. "Georgia Patriots Tell Atheist Group Attacking Prayer: 'Stop Bullying Our Kids.'" *Freedomoutpost.com*. 14 August 2014; n.page. Web.

Boycott the Pledge. "'Under God' compromises patriotic message of the Pledge." *American Humanist Association*. Web.

Buchan, Angus. *Living A Mighty Faith*, Thomas Nelson Publishing: Nashville. 2016. Print.

Casanova, Amanda. "Study: Facebook is Read More Than the Bible." *Christian Headlines.* 5 February 2014; n.page. Web.

Chindamo, Frank. Ed. "Laughter Heals-Laughter Research." *LaughMD, LLC.* 2014; n.page. Web.

Christie, Joel. "The Husband and Wife who died as they lived, inseparably." *Daily Mail.* 3 August 2014; n.page. Web.

Chun, Susan. "Are we born with a moral core? The Baby Lab says 'yes.'" *CNN.* 14 February 2014; n.page. Web

Clarke, Suzan. "Soldier WWII Letter to Wife Found Son 69 Years Later." *Good Morning America.* ABC News. 27 June 3013; n.page. Web.

CNN Wire Staff, "Weiner apologizes for lying 'terrible mistakes,' refuses to resign." *CNN Politics.* 7 June 2011; n.page. Web.

Dailymail. "This Devoted Father Carries His Son 18 Miles to School Every Day. Refuses to Give Up On Him." *Sunnyskyz.* 11 March 2014; n.page. Web.

Dano, Buddy. "Words of Wisdom by Theodore Roosovelt." The Divine Viewpoint. 2005; n.page. Web.

Dice, Mark. "Americans Don't Know Why We Celebrate the 4th of July or What County We Declared Independence From!" Online Video Clip. YouTube. *YouTube.* 1 July 2013; n.page. Web.

DiSalvo, David. "The 10 Reasons Why We Fail." *Forbes.* 7 August 2012; n.page. Web.

Dwight D. Eisenhower Presidential Library, Museum and Boyhood Home. "Dwight D. Eisenhower, 1953 Presidential Inauguration." National Archives and Records Administration.2016; n.page. Web.

Farstad, Art. "The Bible and the Presidents." *Grace Evangelical Society*. February 1992; n.page. Web

Fea, John. "America Has Always Been a Christian Nation." *Patheos Evangelical*. 8 December 2010; n.page. Web.

Empower Yourself with Color Psychology. "The Color White." 2016; n.page. Web

"Establishment Clause." Cornell University Law School. 2016; n.page. Web.

Get Beyond. "Story Behind the Hymn – Tis So Sweet to Trust in Jesus." Online video clip. *YouTube*. YouTube, 17 April 2011. Web.

Got Questions Ministries. "Why is God going to give us a white stone with a new name?" 2016; n.page. Web.

Gryboski, Michael. "New Jersey Teen Heads to Court to Defend Her Right to Say 'Under God' in Pledge of Allegiance." *The Christian Post*. 2 September 2014; n.page. Web.

Hall, Mimi. "For Rep Antony Weiner, a dramatic fall via social media." *USA Today*. 7 July 2011; n.page. Web.

Hallowell, Billy. "Cheerleader's Bold Move During a Moment of Silence That Led Hundred to Chant in Unison Following Prayer Ban." *The Blaze*. September 19, 2014; n.page. Web.

Hennessey, Michael. "Man Celebrates birthday every year by giving out $5 bills in the Triad." *Fox 8 News*. Updated 4 September 2014; n.page. Web.

"John Barrymore." *AZQuotes.com*. Wind and Fly LTD, 2016. 4 October 2016; n.page. Web.

Johnson, Ciatlin. "Cutting Through Advertising Clutter." *CBS, Sunday Morning*. 17 September 2006; n.page. Web

Jones, Laurie Beth. *Jesus, CEO: Using Ancient Wisdom for Visionary Leadership*. Hachette Books, 2001. Print.

Joseph, Dan. "Student Sign Petition to Legalize 4th Trimester Abortion." Online Video Clip. YouTube. *MRCTV.org*. 25 July 2013. Web.

Katzeff, Paul. "Basketball Player Larry Bird Grit and Discipline Helped Him Lead Championship Teams." *Investor's Business Daily News*. January 31, 2001; n.page. Web.

Key, Francis Scott. "The Star Spangled Banner Lyrics." *USA Flag Site*. 2016; n.page. Web.

Klinghoffer, David. "Intelligent Design's Secret Weapon: The World." Discovery Institute. October 15, 2014; n.page. Web.

LaMendola, Chris. "Slow Fade by Casting Crowns with Lyrics." Online video clip. *YouTube*. YouTube, 26 March 2009. Web.

LeClaire, Jennifer. "Facebook Takes Place of Bible in Most American's Lives." *Charisma*. 5 February 2014; n.page. Web.

Leff, Alex. Osterman, Cynthia, Ed. "Til 2013 do us part? Mexico mulls 2-year marriage." Reuters. 29 September 2011; n.page. Web.

Lewis, C. S. *Reflections*. C. S. Lewis Institute. 2006. PDF File. Web.

Malachowski, Dan and Jon Simonini. "Wasted Time At Work Still Costing Companies Billions in 2006." *Salary.com.* 2006; n.page. Web.

Maxwell, John C. *Failing Upwards.* Thomas Nelson Publishers: Nashville. 2000. Print.

Maxwell, John C. *The 21 Irrefutable Laws of Leadership.* Thomas Nelson Publishers: Nashville. 1998. Print.

Maxwell, John C. *Thinking For A Change.* Thomas Nelson Publishers: Nashville. 2000. Print.

Murashko, Alex. "InterVarsity Christian Fellowship Forced to 'Reinvent' College Campus Ministry Due to CSU Non-Discrimination Policy." *The Christian Post.* 10 September 2014; n.page. Web

Ourdocuments.gov. Franklin Roosevelt's D-Day Prayer." National Archives and Records Administration. "2016; n.page. Web.

National Geographic. "Too Much Pot." Online Video Clip. Alaska State Troopers. *National Geographic* . 4 March 2013; n.page. Web.

Orme, Brian. "Abby Is No Longer Here But Her Final Message Will Inspire Your Faith in a Million Ways." *Faithit.* September 2013; n.page. Web.

Orme, Brian. "Dad with Cancer Writes 826 Napkin Notes to Inspire His Daughter Every Day of High School." *Faithit.* September 2013; n.page. Web.

Orme, Brian. "I've Never Seen an Airline Do Anything Like This. These Passengers Got the Surprise of a Lifetime." Online video clip. *Faithit.* Web. 2016

Plushnick-Mash, Ramit. "Texas Teens Fatal DWI Defence: Affluenza." *USA Today.* 12 December 2013; n.page. Web.

Rankin, Russ. "Study: Bible Engagement in Churchgoers' Hearts, Not Always Practiced." LifeWay Christian Resources. 2016; n.page. Web.

"Reagan's Remarks on Prayer." *The New York Times.* 7 May 1982; n.page. Web. 5 October 2016. Transcription.

Selby, John. *Stonewall Jackson as Military Commander.* Barnes & Noble Inc. 2000. Print.

Starnes, Todd. "Atty: Library Removes Christian-themed Books." *Fox News Radio.* 2014: n.page. Web.

Starnes, Todd. "Military Bars Troops from Attending Vacation Bible School Honor." *Fox News Opinion.* 25 July 2014: n.page. Web.

Stewart, Ryan. "11 Bonhoeffer Quotes to Remember a Pastor Who Resisted Evil Unto Death." *Sojourners.* 8 April 2016: n.page. Web.

Strobel, Lee. "About Lee. Author. Apologist. Evangelist." 2016; n.page. Web

"Watch What Garth Brooks Does After Spotting A Woman's Sign in the Audience." Online Video Clip. YouTube. *SunnySkyz.* 7 November 2014; n.page. Web.

Torres, Hazel. "Finding God in girl's secret letter to her future self: Emotions stirred anew as social media users share her inspiring story." *Christian Today*. 28 June 2016: n.page. Web.

Thomasch, Paul "Quick quiz: How much TV do Americans watch?" *Reuters*. 26 March 2010; n.page. Web.

"You'll Cry When She Sees Soldier Dad." *CNN*. Online Video Clip. 2016. Web.

"Van Orden v. Perry (2005)." Cornell University Law School; n.page. Web

Wexler, Harry K. "A Cure for Divorce: Term Marital Contracts." *Psychology Today*. August 20, 2009: n.page. Web.

Wong, Brittany. "Couple has An Open Marriage So Complicated It's Hard to Keep Track." *Then Huffington Post*. 26 November 2013: n.page. Web. Updated 10 November 2014.

Woolley, John and Gerhad Peters. "Presidential Debate in Baltimore (Reagan-Anderson)." *The American Presidency Project*. 2016: n.page. Web.

Woolley, John and Gerhad Peters. "Proclamation 97-Appointing a Day of National Humiliation, Fasting, and Prayer." *The American Presidency Project*. 2016. n.page. Web.

# About the Author

Dr. Robert M. Myers has been a part of Christian higher education since 1993 and currently serves as the seventh President of Toccoa Falls College.

Dr. Myers has not only served in educational institutions; he has served as a police officer from 1976-1988, in Maryland, where he held various assignments including patrol officer, field training officer, polygraph examiner, SCUBA team member, hostage negotiator, and detective.

Dr. Myers served as a manuscript reviewer for the Academy of Management (Management History Division). He also served as a reviewer for both Prentice Hall and McGraw-Hill. His publications are included in academic journals such as *Informatica, Management Decision, The Journal of the Association of Marketing Educators, Florida Banker,* as well as proceedings from many national and International conferences.

Dr. Myers was also ranked as one of the top twelve most prolific writing college presidents in the country producing a large number of written opinion pieces. He is also a regular blogger for the Huffington Post, representing the conservative Christian position on cultural issues of the day.

Dr. Myers is a native of Torrance, California but spent many of his formative years in Pennsylvania and Maryland where he attended The Mercersburg Academy and subsequently received a Bachelor of Science degree from The University of Maryland. Dr. Myers also holds an M.B.A from Palm Beach Atlantic University and a D.B.A from Nova Southeastern University.

He and his wife, Cheri, have two children, Joshua and Joy.

www.ingramcontent.com/pod-product-compliance
Lightning Source LLC
LaVergne TN
LVHW051301080426
835509LV00020B/3096